39.95

D1717025

Chickamauga

Chickamauga

A BATTLEFIELD HISTORY IN IMAGES

Roger C. Linton

The University of Georgia Press

Athens and London

© 2004 by the University of Georgia Press
Athens, Georgia 30602

Designed by April Leidig-Higgins
Set in Ehrhardt by Copperline Book Services, Inc.
Printed and bound by Everbest for Four Colour Imports

The paper in this book meets the guidelines for permanence
and durability of the Committee on Production Guidelines
for Book Longevity of the Council on Library Resources.

Printed in China
08 07 06 05 04 C 5 4 3 2 1

Library of Congress Cataloging-in-Publication Data
Linton, Roger C., 1943–
Chickamauga : a battlefield history in images / Roger C. Linton.
p. cm.
Includes bibliographical references (p.) and index.
ISBN 0-8203-2598-8 (hardcover : alk. paper)
1. Chickamauga, Battle of, Ga., 1863—Pictorial works.
2. Chickamauga Battlefield (Ga.)—Pictorial works. I. Title.
E475.81.L56 2004
973.7'34—dc22
2003023679

British Library Cataloging-in-Publication Data available

To the memory of my mother and father

"As we moved along the road leading to the Widow Glenn's house, from a ridge overlooking the valley of the Chickamauga, we could see the smoke of battle rising above the trees almost shutting out our view of the forest. . . . We could see part of General McCook's corps, numbering perhaps ten to twelve thousand men, including artillery, moving at double quick time down into the woods, out of which were pouring thousands of wounded soldiers and stragglers. It was a sight never to be forgotten."

—from *History of the Seventy-Eighth Pennsylvania Volunteer Infantry*, by J. T. Gibson

CONTENTS

MAPS

In September 1863, two armies met on a field of battle in rural northwest Georgia and departed, leaving a wake of death, destruction, and memories of valor that can never be forgotten. Those memories of the campaign and battle named Chickamauga remained etched in the minds of those who fought there and culminated in the creation of the first National Military Park, encompassing much of the Chickamauga battlefield and many sites of the subsequent battles for Chattanooga. Chickamauga remains historically categorized as the bloodiest battle in the western theater of the Civil War for the major combat of September 19–20, 1863, and the heavy localized fighting at Reed's and Alexander's bridges on the so-called "River of Death" on September 18.

This collection of historical photographic and artistic print images related to the battle of Chickamauga is intended as a representative visual record of the battlefield, supplemented by modern photographs for comparison. No such effort could be attempted with only the contemporaneous Civil War photographs of this particular battlefield, since few were recorded or survived. The richest source of battlefield photographs approximating the appearance of the landscape as seen by the soldiers who fought there is located in the archives of views recorded around the time the Chickamauga and Chattanooga National Military Park was opened in 1895. Additionally, the growing popularity of postcards featuring photographic images in the late nineteenth and early twentieth centuries led to increased interest in and photographic recording of images of scenic views, including battlefields.

It is the intent of this book to include visual images of all the prominent sites on Chickamauga battlefield. For those sites of which no revealing photographs were found, or where the view of the site is enhanced by creative representations, selected prints of notable artists of the period are provided, including works by Alfred R. Waud, William Waud, Frank Vizetelly, and Thomas Nash. Where possible or informative for differences in the landscape, contemporary photographs were taken from a similar perspective as the period photographs.

Text and captioning for each site explain the historical context of the views and the comparative changes in the appearance of the battlefield since 1863. The order of sites included in the text, with accompanying images, is developed for a suggested driving route following park roads from the Visitor Center, with some backtracking necessary for visiting sites in the approximate chronology of the battle.

Aerial Photomap of Chickamauga Battlefield

(Sites numbered for identification purposes only)

1. Visitor Center—Site of McDonald House
2. Position of Dan McCook's Brigade on September 18–19
3. Site of Jay's Mill
4. Site of Bragg's Headquarters on September 20
5. Winfrey Field
6. Position of Van Derveer's Brigade on September 19
7. Preston Smith and Seventy-seventh Pennsylvania Monuments
8. Brock Field
9. John Ingraham Grave
10. Kelly Farm—Battle Line Road
11. Poe Farm
12. Brotherton Farm
13. West Brock Field
14a. East Viniard Field
14b. West Viniard Field
15. Widow Glenn's Farm— Wilder Tower
16. Bloody Pond
17a. Dyer Farm—Lytle Hill— Tan Yard
17b. North Dyer Field
18. Snodgrass Farm
19. Horseshoe Ridge
20. Site of Vittetoe House
21. Tennessee Artillery Monument

Directions indicated to:
McFarland's Gap
Rossville Gap—Ross House
Reed's Bridge
Lee & Gordon's Mill

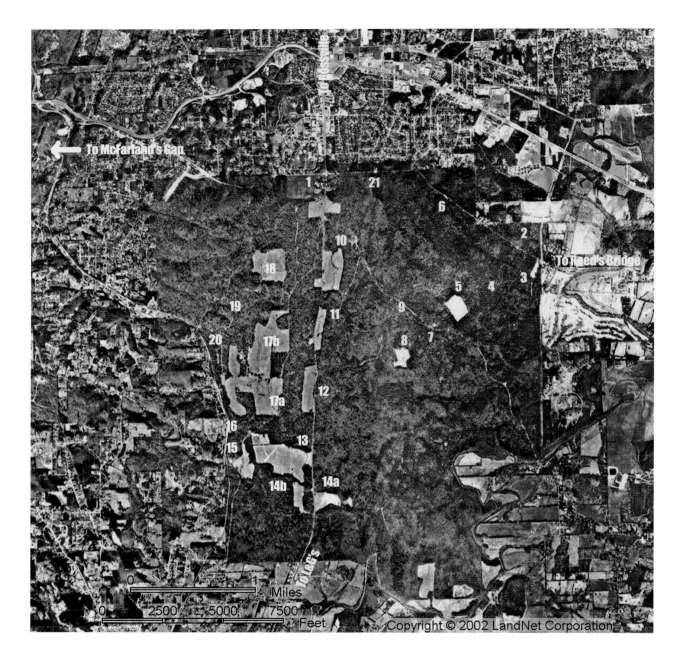

ACKNOWLEDGMENTS

I am very grateful to all of the contributing individuals and institutions for photographic and print images used in this work. Particularly deserving of mention for pleasant and generous help are Gladys Dailey Nevels for the "Lost Corner School" photograph; Robert D. Gunnels, Associate Vice-Chancellor for Instruction, Southern Arkansas University Tech, for the image of an operating steam sawmill; Dan Hatzenbuehler for "Morton's Battery"; and Lisa Bayne, curator, Eli Lilly and Company, for the image of Eli Lilly revisiting the battlefield. The staffs of the libraries of Huntsville, Chattanooga, UTC-Chattanooga, Chickamauga and Chattanooga National Military Park, and the Tennessee State Museum were very helpful in my searches for archival manuscripts, books, and images.

I am indebted to the artists and photographers of the nineteenth and early twentieth centuries, and those whose work combines the artistry of both professions. The latter category includes the modern work of Emmett Given, whose enthusiasm, untiring patience, and professionalism successfully combined the objectives of both scenic composition and historical relevance. I gratefully acknowledge the inspiration from books by James Frassanito, whose original works of battlefield interpretation encourage all who favor the "then and now" approach. I would like to thank Henry Marks, author, historian, and friend, for his invaluable critiques of earlier work that inspired me to continue. Special mention is due Ed Tinney, former historian at Chickamauga and Chattanooga National Military Park; former staff ranger Woody Harrell; and former Eastern National manager Bob Housch, whose help and suggestions in earlier years contributed much to my understanding of and enthusiasm for the battlefield.

James Ogden III, chief historian at Chickamauga and Chattanooga National Military Park, was particularly helpful in researching historical photographs and in answering a multitude of questions. The park interpretive staff, particularly Hugh Odom and Lee White, and Eastern National personnel James Jolly, Marie Harris, and Richard Manion were always helpful on my many visits.

The sustained and very helpful support of the staff of the University of Georgia Press, particularly Associate Director and Editor in Chief Nancy Grayson, Managing Editor Jennifer Reichlin, and Project Editor Jon Davies, is deeply appreciated.

This book could not have been completed without the love and generous support of my wife, Ilene, my daughter, Shelly, and her husband, Donald, and my son, David, and his wife, Marcia.

Chickamauga

The Battle of Chickamauga

Through the summer and fall of 1863, Chattanooga, Tennessee, with a population of only 2,500, became the central focus of the Civil War. As a key rail and communications center, a crucial junction in the dwindling Confederate supply chain, this Gateway to Georgia and the Heartland of the South had become foremost in strategic importance to both sides in the conflict. The Tullahoma campaign, launched in late June 1863, was the first phase of military operations ultimately aimed at Chattanooga, at a time when the siege of Vicksburg to the west and Lee's invasion of Pennsylvania to the north neared resolution. In central Tennessee, Major General William S. Rosecrans, commanding the Union Army of the Cumberland, set his troops in motion from bases near Murfreesboro. General Braxton Bragg, commander of the Confederate Army of Tennessee, had situated his men astride the direct approaches south.

Their armies had last fought six months earlier at Stone's River, Tennessee. The Union declared victory when the Confederate army withdrew on January 2, after three days of intense, intermittent fighting. Although the Confederates now held strongly fortified positions at Tullahoma and Shelbyville, they were heavily outnumbered, and Rosecrans skillfully executed a series of flanking maneuvers that compelled Bragg's army to abandon the Tullahoma defenses and withdraw from nearly all of Middle Tennessee, crossing the Tennessee River into the city of Chattanooga.

Within the seemingly impregnable natural defenses of the city girded by Lookout Mountain to the west and the river in front, Bragg entrenched his army, focusing his attention on the river crossings to the northeast. Rosecrans's carefully orchestrated demonstrations of force had deceived Bragg into believing the Union army would attack there. Early in September, Rosecrans once again outwitted his Confederate counterpart as the Union army crossed the Tennessee River unopposed southwest of the city, forcing Bragg to again withdraw southward to protect his supply lines against a reported widespread Union advance to the south. Union infantry forces occupied the evacuated city of Chattanooga on September 9, only one day behind the retreating Confederate army.

As Rosecrans's strategy unfolded and the Union army broke into three elements of command to facilitate the crossings of Lookout Mountain, Bragg secretly concentrated his forces at LaFayette, Georgia, twenty-six miles south of Chattanooga. Heavy reinforcements from east Tennessee, Mississippi, and Virginia were en route; two infantry brigades had arrived in late August. Among the last to arrive would be forward units of two divisions of Lieutenant General James Longstreet's three-division corps of Lee's Army of Northern Virginia, dispatched from Richmond on September 9 along a diverted coastal route of some eight hundred miles of rickety, makeshift rail lines. After two unsuccessful attempts to attack and destroy detached elements of the widely dispersed Union army, Bragg moved his forces north to cross Chickamauga Creek, attack the Union left stationed at Lee and Gordon's Mill, and seize the approaches to Chattanooga. He was unaware that Rosecrans had sensed the danger and ordered his forces to concentrate near the same point the Confederate army was approaching, with only Major General Gordon Granger's small corps held in reserve near Chattanooga.

By September 18, advance forces of the Confederate army had marched downstream and, despite fierce skirmishing with outlying Union patrols, they occupied the key fords, moving into positions east of the Chickamauga.

On the morning of September 19, an advance detachment of Union infantry struck a reconnaissance patrol of Confederate cavalry at Jay's Mill, near the

Reed's Bridge crossing of Chickamauga Creek, and opened the battle of Chickamauga. Fighting spread south along a widening four-mile front as the commanders on both sides, hampered by the heavily wooded terrain, reacted instinctively by feeding in successive reinforcements the moment they arrived on the scene. In desperate fighting throughout the day, the Confederates succeeded only in forcing the Union army back into a final defensive line along the LaFayette Road.

The next morning the battle resumed with Bragg's army following the original strategy of turning the Union left and seizing the roads to Chattanooga. Rosecrans's forces held firm until a gap opened in the right-center of the Union lines at the Brotherton farm and Lieutenant General James Longstreet's Confederates broke through, sweeping the right wing and part of the center from the field. Union General George Thomas rallied a jumble of isolated units on the steep heights of Snodgrass Hill and withstood Longstreet's relentless attacks throughout the remaining hours of daylight. As darkness approached, Thomas withdrew his remaining Union forces through McFarland's Gap to the safety of occupied Chattanooga.

The battle culminated in the greatest victory of Confederate arms in the western theater of the Civil War. Reinforced Confederate forces totaling some sixty-six thousand men had defeated an opposing Union army fielding no more than fifty-eight thousand. For a brief time, in the aftermath of devastating earlier losses at Vicksburg and Gettysburg, new hopes were raised for Southern independence. Yet in the end, the Confederates' failure to oust the Union army from their newly secured strongholds in the captured city of Chattanooga would nullify this great success.

Chickamauga Battlefield

The battle fought in West Chickamauga Valley on September 19 and 20, 1863, culminated in Confederate victory, at a fearful cost in lives on both sides, and proved to be the largest battle fought in the western theater of the Civil War. Overshadowed for generations by the attention devoted to the conflict in the East, the battlefields of Chickamauga and the subsequent battles for Chattanooga were nonetheless among the first commemorated as national military

parks. Chickamauga and Chattanooga National Military Park became, in fact, the first of its kind, established by an act of Congress on August 19, 1890. The park was dedicated on September 19, 1895, at the foot of Snodgrass Hill, with Vice President Adlai E. Stevenson providing the opening address. The Chattanooga fields of battle were dedicated the following day in the city that had been the focus of all the fighting, inside a great tent provided by the secretary of war, with a seating capacity exceeding ten thousand.[1]

General Ferdinand Van Derveer, who served as a colonel commanding a brigade of the Union Army of the Cumberland at Chickamauga, and Lieutenant Colonel Henry Van Ness Boynton, a regimental commander under Van Derveer in the battle, deserve major credit for the idea of preserving the fields of battle at Chickamauga and Chattanooga. Stimulated by a return visit to the scenes of battle at Chickamauga in 1888, Van Derveer wrote to his fellow veterans: "The survivors of the Army of the Cumberland should awake to great pride in this notable field of Chickamauga. Why should it not, as well as eastern fields, be marked by monuments, and its lines be accurately preserved for history? There was no more magnificent fighting during the war than both armies did there. Both sides might well unite in preserving the field where both, in a military sense, won such renown."[2]

Both sides did unite in the rapidly evolving campaign to purchase lands and mark the battle lines with monuments and markers. Beginning in 1889, Confederate and Union veterans of the battle worked enthusiastically together in the Joint Chickamauga Memorial Association, an outgrowth of the groundwork laid by the Society of the Army of the Cumberland. These battlefields would set precedent with the marking of both Union and Confederate positions. While monuments had been placed on the Gettysburg battlefield commencing from 1863, only Union positions and actions had been commemorated.

In the words of the 1890 congressional legislation establishing the creation of the Chickamauga and Chattanooga National Military Park, the purposes were: "preserving and suitably marking for historical and professional military study the fields of some of the most remarkable maneuvers and most brilliant fighting in the war of the rebellion." The plan was to restore the battlefields to the same condition as existed at the time of the battles, within practical limits. Fifteen square miles of Georgia and Tennessee lands were purchased for incorporation, with the largest area, approximately eight thousand acres, included in Chickamauga battlefield.

Within three years of the formal dedication of the battlefield, other uses for the substantial acreage included in the National Military Park were implemented. The War Department had supervised the creation of the park, and military training exercises had been intermittently conducted on the battlefield grounds since 1866. The outbreak of the Spanish-American War in 1898 brought thousands of American soldiers to the hastily improvised Camp George H. Thomas, including the famous black regiments known as the Buffalo Soldiers. The soldiers and recruits were transported in by rail and housed on the battlefield for training. Despite rampant disease among the recruits, which led to greater casualties than suffered throughout the fighting in Cuba, the site proved highly effective as a training camp.

In the aftermath of the relatively short war, plans were formulated for a permanent facility adjacent to the battlefield park grounds. Fort Oglethorpe was established in 1902. With the outbreak of World War I, an influx of some sixty thousand recruits overwhelmed the limited facilities, and some sixteen hundred barracks and supply buildings were erected, extending over the grounds of the battlefield park. Nearly all traces of these training camps were subsequently removed, at least to the eye of the casual observer.

The park would remain under the jurisdiction of the War Department until 1933, when authority was permanently transferred to the civilian National Park Service. Chickamauga and Chattanooga National Military Park remains true to its original purposes of "preserving and suitably marking for historical and professional military study" the fields of battle while conducting landscape management in the context of evolving historical understanding.

THE LANDSCAPE AND MARKING of the battlefield have changed in the years since the opening of the park. Texas provided its state monument in 1964, honoring native soldiers who fought in the battles of Chickamauga and Chattanooga. The National Park Service placed the Texas state monument along Battle Line Road, in the vicinity of heavy fighting by Texas regiments of Brigadier General James Deshler's infantry brigade. In 1977, Brigadier General Bushrod R. Johnson's contributions to the battle of Chickamauga were recog-

nized in the dedication of the most recent monument on the battlefield, placed on the Brotherton Road along the route of his infantry division's advance to the Brotherton farm. A major addition to the park Visitor Center/administration complex, including a multimedia presentation theater, was dedicated in 1990. By the year 2001, park clearing operations at the Viniard farm site had removed some of the regrowth timber that, for many years, obscured the open views of the Viniard farm fields recorded in late nineteenth century photographs.

The Chickamauga battlefield as it is seen today is the result of the plans and accomplishments of those who have developed and those who have overseen the national park. The following is extracted from an 1895 historical guide to the Chickamauga and Chattanooga National Military Park by Boynton, a regimental commander at the rank of colonel under Van Derveer during the battle of Chickamauga and a prominent leader in the evolution and creation of the park: "Except in the growth of timber, the features of the Chickamauga field have changed but little since the battle. There have been few clearings in the extensive woods where the heavy fighting occurred, but several of the fields in these forests had grown up with heavy timber."[3] One of the reasons for the lack of extensive forest clearing was the prevalence of imbedded iron shot and shell in the trees of certain areas that reportedly ruined the blades of local sawmills, leading to a refusal to accept logs cut from the battlefield. One area of the battlefield where extensive postwar clearing significantly altered the landscape was the site of Jay's Mill, where the battle opened on September 19.[4]

Boynton and other veterans who returned to study the topography of the lines of battle at first found the effort "quite puzzling." The evolving plan of park creators included clearing recent growths of timber and replanting other areas that had, in fact, regrown since the battle. Boynton writes, "The old roads, which were those of the battle, have been reopened and improved, and roads opened since the battle have been closed and abandoned. The only natural feature existing at the time of the fight, which has been changed, is the cutting out of the underbrush . . . to bring the lines of battle into view, and to show the topography of the field. As a result of this work, carriages can now drive in all directions through the great forests and along the various lines of battle."[5]

In a move intended to emphasize the seriousness of the "professional military study" phrasing in the 1890 congressional act, five iron and steel observation towers, each seventy feet in height to the upper platform, were erected at prominent locations across Chickamauga battlefield and Missionary Ridge. Observers could follow the flow of tactical movements during the battle from three towers located near, respectively, Hall's Ford, where the Confederate army first formed for battle; Jay's Mill, where the fighting began; and Snodgrass Hill, overlooking the scenes of the climactic final struggle. All of these towers have long since been dismantled and removed.

Lines of battle were marked both by monuments and historical tablets. The U.S. government assumed responsibility for the monuments to the regular regiments and batteries, and all of the tablets. The twenty-nine states, northern and southern, that provided troops during the battle were responsible for erecting monuments marking the positions of volunteer organizations.

Several hundred historical tablets, with raised lettering, were distributed across the battlefield, marking the locations and movements of army headquarters, corps, divisions, and brigades. The text was derived from the contributed recollections of veterans who fought there and who returned to pinpoint the various positions. Additionally, locality tablets were erected to designate the sites of houses and fields that became landmarks in the battle, sites where prominent officers were wounded and where notable captures of prisoners or guns occurred. The lettering of these tablets is now painted blue for Union positions and red for Confederate.

Three of the landmark family homes of local settlers are represented on the battlefield today; several others were destroyed by fire during the battle. Reconstructions of the Kelly, Brotherton, and Snodgrass cabins are keystone attractions of the battlefield. The original Kelly house is known to have been destroyed by fire during the battle, though original timber remains in the Brotherton and the Snodgrass cabins.

The fighting positions of all artillery batteries, numbering thirty-five Union and thirty-nine Confederate, have been designated by surviving cannon of the same type used in the battle by each respective battery, mounted on cast-iron carriages selected as authentic representations of the period type.

Eight triangular pyramids of eight-inch shell, ten feet in height, are located at the sites across the battlefield where general officers, or those temporarily exercising the command of general officers, were killed or mortally wounded in action. These include the four Union brigadiers: Colonel Philemon P. Baldwin, Colonel Hans C. Heg, Colonel Edward A. King, and Brigadier General William H. Lytle, and the four Confederate brigade commanders: Colonel Peyton H. Colquitt, Brigadier General Benjamin H. Helm, Brigadier General James Deshler, and Brigadier General Preston Smith.

All of the known lines of each day's battle were marked. At the smallest designated organizational level, regimental monuments were erected where the representatives of particular regiments believed they had contributed the most notable effect. Other positions of note have been designated by small granite markers.

The Photographic Legacy

The historical photographic legacy of Chickamauga battlefield is largely derived from turn-of-the-century images produced at the time of the opening of the National Military Park and the landscape restoration. Few images of scenes associated with the battle of Chickamauga were recorded or survived from the Civil War era, although a thorough record exists of nearly all of the scenes of the subsequent battles for Chattanooga. The most famous of the handful of wartime photographs from Chickamauga is the Mathew Brady image of Lee and Gordon's Mill on Chickamauga Creek (see page 11).

Despite the best efforts and intentions of the park creators, some of the battle scenes photographed in the turn-of-the-century era only approximated the appearance of the landscape the soldiers fought over in 1863. Regrowth of timber, cutting of timber, and the decay and removal of the wrecked timber all affected the appearance of the landscape.

To a significant degree this was a natural consequence of the devastation inflicted during the fighting. J. T. Trowbridge described some of the damage in his *Picture of the Desolated States,* a work based on visits throughout the South in the immediate aftermath of the war: "Driving southward along the LaFayette Road . . . we came to traces of the conflict, —boughs broken and trees cut off by shells . . . the woods beyond, all shattered and torn by shot and shell, as if a tornado had swept them."[6]

Veterans who fought at Chickamauga even differed in their descriptions of the terrain. Some described a forest matted with briar-laced underbrush hindering movement and visibility, while others told of a forest nearly free of undergrowth, with visibility limited only by the towering trees. They were probably both correct in their observations, since the character of the battlefield included large tracts of towering, old-growth timber, particularly on the east side of the LaFayette Road, interspersed with cedar groves, where visibility ranged up to 150 paces. Scattered through the dense forest were several cleared fields belonging to the early settlers who were only beginning to develop their tracts. West of the LaFayette Road, the approximate dividing line of the armies on the second day of battle, larger tracts of open fields were commonplace in 1863. Today, most of these large open fields remain, although heavy regrowth of trees on the borders has obscured some views. In recent years, clearing operations at the park have reopened some important areas, with views now approximating the scenes photographed at the turn of the century and as described by the veterans who fought there.

One of the most striking vistas no longer available is that photographed at the turn of the century from Snodgrass Hill, on the northern end of the battlefield, overlooking the approach route of Union reinforcements at a critical time in the battle on September 20, 1863. Granger's reserve infantry from Rossville had moved towards the embattled forces of Major General George Thomas on Snodgrass Hill through the open fields of the McDonald and Mullis farms, raising long columns of dust from the parched furrows. Panoramic views of the approach route were once available from the tower then standing at the crest of Snodgrass Hill. The tower has long since been removed, and the distant view is now blocked by heavy growth of tall trees.

Other differences in the terrain will be mentioned where appropriate in the text. The National Park Service of the Department of the Interior continuously reviews the battlefield for maintenance, and what visitors see today is a rare and stunning area of natural beauty remarkably true in overall appearance to the field of battle in 1863.

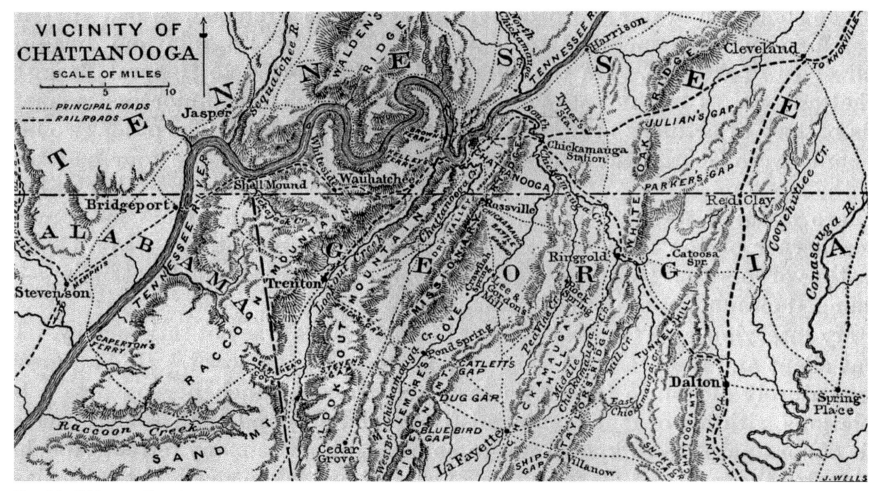

Map of the Chickamauga Campaign

Gordon-Lee House

Major General William Rosecrans and Brigadier General James Garfield, Rosecrans's chief of staff, occupied what later became known as the Gordon-Lee House as headquarters for the Union army of the Cumberland from September 16 through the morning hours of September 19, 1863. The mansion's central location overlooking Crawfish Springs along the route of the Dry Valley road facilitated coordination of the massive troop movement via McClemore's Cove to interpose forces between Bragg's Confederate army and Chattanooga.

By September 17, nearly all of the previously widely dispersed elements of the army were concentrated east of Steven's Gap in Lookout Mountain. Intelligence revealed that Bragg's army was moving farther north from the vicinity of LaFayette, threatening to outflank the Union army and envelop the isolated three divisions of Major General Thomas L. Crittenden's XXI Army Corps near Lee and Gordon's Mill. On the following day, Rosecrans redirected the concentration to the north, above the mill, with Thomas's XIV Corps in the lead. As the battle developed on September 19, Rosecrans shifted headquarters to the Widow Glenn's cabin, closer to the fighting, and the Gordon-Lee House and grounds were used as the main field-hospital complex through both days of battle.[1] Cavalry units were stationed in the immediate vicinity for protection, defending the extreme right flank of the army. After the collapse of the Union right on September 20, ambulances and supply wagons hastily evacuated wounded soldiers, following the Dry Valley road through McFarland's Gap to Chattanooga. In the rush to evacuate, Union forces left many of their wounded, including many too severely injured for transport, behind with rations and medical supplies. Several surgeons and other medical personnel remained to care for these and the thousands of Union wounded left on the battlefield, in the custody of their Confederate captors.[2]

DIRECTIONS: From the Visitor Center, drive approximately 3.5 miles south on the LaFayette Road to the intersection with U.S. 27. Turn left and proceed to the stoplight intersection of Lee and Gordon's Mill Road. Turn right, proceed approximately 0.8 mile and turn left onto Crittenden Avenue, bearing to the right as it becomes West Tenth Street. Turn left again at the stoplight intersection of Cove Road (marked as Gordon to the right). The nearby site is prominently marked on the right, and the grounds are available to the public for inspection (at a fee).

Gordon-Lee House

Field headquarters of the Army of the Cumberland were located at the Widow Gordon's brick mansion overlooking Crawfish Springs from September 16 through the morning of September 19. James Gordon, who founded in 1836 the nearby gristmill bearing his name, completed construction of his home in 1847. By the 1860s, Gordon's son-in-law James Lee operated the mill and acquired ownership of all of the family property sometime after the death of James Gordon in 1863. When Rosecrans departed on September 19 for a site closer to the battle developing to the north, the house and grounds became the principal field-hospital complex for the Union army.

In the days preceding the battle near Chickamauga Creek, Rosecrans conferred with his staff and top commanders in the parlor of his stately headquarters, while the evicted family purportedly adjusted to life in one of the six adjacent slave quarters.[3]

Crawfish Springs

Union soldiers arriving at the site of the Widow Gordon's mansion in September 1863, after grueling forced marches through the heat of drought-stricken north Georgia, wrote glowing reports of filling canteens from the cold, clear waters of adjacent Crawfish Springs.[4] The water gushed from a subterranean spring at the base of a high bank where the route of the Dry Valley road passed north to McFarland's Gap. On the night of September 19, Union soldiers of the Thirty-ninth Indiana Mounted Infantry Regiment brought hundreds of canteens filled with the spring water to the troops on the field near the Widow Glenn's farm.

Lee and Gordon's Mill

In September 1863, Lee and Gordon's Mill became the focus of Union and Confederate strategy in the preliminary maneuvering for position. General Bragg's headquarters was located at the site from September 7 until late on the tenth, when the Confederate commander relocated his center of operations to LaFayette, closer to the scene of a developing confrontation in McClemore's Cove. From September 10–19, Major General Thomas L. Crittenden, commanding the XXI Corps of the Union army, maintained headquarters at the site, while skirmishes flared with Confederate cavalry and infantry outposts as the combined forces of both armies neared. As early as September 12, Bragg turned from his subordinate generals' failure to surround and destroy an isolated Union force in McClemore's Cove and refocused efforts towards Lee and Gordon's Mill, where only one of Crittenden's three infantry divisions faced the approaching columns of Lieutenant General Leonidas Polk's Confederate Corps. Crittenden managed to reunite his corps by rapid forced marches through the night from the vicinity of Ringgold before Bragg's scheduled attack at dawn on the thirteenth. Polk then refused to attack the fortified heights in his front, even when Major General Simon B. Buckner's Corps was moved up in support. General Bragg, with intense frustration, suspended major operations through September 17 while awaiting further reinforcements.

With the arrival of leading elements of Longstreet's infantry beginning on September 17, Bragg launched his major envelopment of Crittenden's position on September 18, unaware of the approaching columns of Union infantry then moving up the Dry Valley road to the west.[1]

By the morning of September 19, with Confederate infantry moving into position to strike from both sides of the Chickamauga, Crittenden retained Brigadier General Thomas Wood's First Division on the bluff at the mill, while deploying his other two divisions one mile northward along the line of the LaFayette Road. The flow of reinforcements from both armies to the developing battle to the north gradually drew in all of Crittenden's units. Major General Philip Sheridan's Third Division of Major General Alexander McCook's XX Corps arrived from the south in the early afternoon and crossed Chickamauga Creek at the mill, virtually completing the concentration of the Union army; two of Sheridan's three brigades were dispatched late in the afternoon to the scene where heavy fighting had seemingly ebbed at the Viniard farm.[2]

By the morning of September 20, the site of Lee and Gordon's Mill stood virtually abandoned by both armies as Confederate forces attacked consolidated Union lines farther north. Major General Joseph Wheeler's Confederate cavalry took possession of the mill in the late afternoon, after battling Union cavalry and infantry units protecting the withdrawal of the final trains of supply wagons and ambulances.[3]

DIRECTIONS: From the Visitor Center, drive four miles south on the LaFayette Road to the intersection with the U.S. 27 bypass, then turn left and proceed to the first stoplight. Turn left onto Lee and Gordon's Mill Road and proceed to the intersection of Red Belt Road. Turn right and prepare for an immediate left turn into the site.

Lee and Gordon's Mill

View from south

This Brady Studios photograph of Lee and Gordon's Mill (ca. 1865) remains one of the most identifiable historical images associated with the battle of Chickamauga. The view is to the northeast from the perspective of the high ground in front of the mill, where a branch of the LaFayette Road then diverged east to a nearby bridge crossing Chickamauga Creek. Major General Thomas Wood's infantry division occupied positions along this high ground prior to the opening of battle on September 19. The gristmill operation on West Chickamauga Creek, established by James Gordon in 1836 and later rebuilt and operated with partner James Lee, expanded in time to include a sawmill and a general store.[4]

The second image from the same collection provides a closer view of the structure and adjacent sawmill from the rear, creek side just above the dam.

View from north

Aerial View of Lee and Gordon's Mill

Surviving elements of Lee and Gordon's Mill still stand at the site where James Gordon first erected a water-powered gristmill on Chickamauga Creek in 1836. The original mill was rebuilt in 1857 in partnership with James Lee with the addition of a sawmill and general store. This structure, having suffered no significant damage from skirmishing in the vicinity during the battle of Chickamauga, survived until a reported fire in 1867. James Lee rebuilt the structure that remained in operation, with few interruptions, until 1967. In this aerial view from the northeast (ca. 1985), the high peaked roof of the mill, at lower right center, stands along the meandering course of Chickamauga Creek with the line of the millrace dam visible in the water behind. Nearby at left center is a modern steel and concrete span that replaced the old postwar wooden covered bridge. Monuments on the high ground across the road passing in front of the mill mark positions of Union and Confederate units at different times in the battle. Some, including the shell monument marking the site of the headquarters for Crittenden's Twenty-first Corps along the LaFayette Road to the right, have since been moved closer to the hillside overlooking the mill. The building survived as a deteriorating landmark of the area until new owners restored the structure and reconstructed the site in 1993. The site is privately owned but publicly accessible.[5]

John Ross House at Rossville Gap in Missionary Ridge

Although Rosecrans may have erred in the rapid dispersal of his army through the mountainous north Georgia terrain in pursuit of Bragg's army, he retained one advantage that would prove crucial in the conclusion of the Chickamauga campaign. Major General Gordon Granger's Union reserve corps, with three infantry brigades and part of the army's two cavalry divisions, remained in the vicinity of Rossville Gap, posted to guard the approaches to Chattanooga through Missionary Ridge. On September 17, part of Granger's infantry and cavalry advanced as far as Ringgold in preliminary skirmishing with advance units of the Confederate army. On the following day, Colonel Robert Minty's cavalry defended the approaches to Reed's Bridge over Chickamauga Creek through much of the afternoon until forced to withdraw by Brigadier General Bushrod R. Johnson's infantry and Brigadier General Nathan Bedford Forrest's cavalry. Granger's late deployment of two infantry brigades in support of Minty accomplished little more than the capture of a few Confederate stragglers from Bushrod Johnson's column of march. This led to Colonel Daniel McCook's assumption and report to Thomas that a single Confederate brigade

had crossed and was stranded on the west side of Chickamauga Creek, trapped by what he assumed was the total destruction of Reed's Bridge on the morning of September 19. The recall of these two brigades that morning effectively ended the active role of the reserve corps for the first day of battle, other than heavy skirmishing with detachments of Confederate cavalry at the lower fords of Chickamauga Creek. By noon of the following day, with his infantry poised in positions of readiness near McAfee's Church on the Ringgold Road, Granger's frustration with his standby role in the battle raging less than three miles to the south led to his decision, without direct orders, to march down in support with, initially, the two infantry brigades of Steedman's First Division.[1]

DIRECTIONS: From the Visitor Center, drive north on U.S. 27. Rossville Gap is located approximately three miles beyond the battlefield. At the second stoplight on U.S. 27 past the Iowa state monument and the junction with Crest Road, turn left onto Spring Street, then right onto Lake Road, and immediately left into the posted parking area for the site of the Ross House.

Original Location of John Ross House

Major General Gordon Granger's head-quarters was initially located at the base of Missionary Ridge, near Rossville Gap, at the site of the former home of the Cherokee Chief John Ross. A partial view of the structure, including one of the two chimneys, is visible at the far right in this George N. Barnard image (ca. 1864). In this view to the southeast, the old Federal Road behind the soldier standing near unidentified ruins leads, to the left, through Rossville Gap, passing between the high ground rising above the Ross house and the barren slopes of the north shoulder. For the days preceding and during the battle, base camps for Granger's reserve corps were located south of Missionary Ridge in fields near a site identified as McAfee's Church.[2]

John Ross House

Photographer George Barnard captured this image of the Ross house in the wake of the Union victory at Chattanooga in November 1863. A facade of planking covers the original hand-hewn logs of the house built by Scottish immigrant John McDonald in 1797, at a location originally named Poplar Springs. McDonald's grandson, John Ross, who lived in the house from 1808 to 1827, initially gained fame as cofounder of Ross's Landing on the Tennessee River, the origin of a growing settlement that would later be known as Chattanooga. Long active in the affairs of the regional Cherokee Indians, Ross was elected principal chief by their emerging nation, despite his distant one-eighth Cherokee heritage at birth.[3] Granger established headquarters at the Ross house as the base of operations for his reserve corps protecting the approaches to Chattanooga.

Modern View of Ross House

After more than two hundred years, the John Ross house remains standing at the base of Missionary Ridge in Rossville, Georgia. A relocation in 1962 to a site several hundred feet back from commercial growth along the route of busy U.S. 27, and overlooking a small lake formed by the waters of Poplar Springs, preserved the structure of one of the oldest buildings in north Georgia. The plank facade visible in earlier photographs was removed at the time of the relocation.

Reed's Bridge

In the days immediately preceding battle, General Braxton Bragg prepared to launch a general offensive from the northeast designed to drive much of the widely spread Union army south into McLemore's Cove. Bragg initially planned for a coordinated first strike on September 18 directed at the then isolated Union force near Lee and Gordon's Mill. His detailed plans for rapidly moving a large part of his army to the west side of Chickamauga Creek were delayed by last-minute changes in approach routes and the unexpected resistance of outlying Union infantry and cavalry units. Ordered to cross at Reed's Bridge, Brigadier General Bushrod Johnson's division lost several hours in skirmishing and countermarching before arriving at the gap in Pea Vine Ridge overlooking, at a distance of 1.5 miles, the Reed's Bridge crossing. Colonel Robert Minty's Union cavalry brigade, outnumbered nearly four to one, effectively employed delaying tactics that forced Johnson to deploy his thirty-six hundred troops in line of battle and climb over the steep heights of the ridge. Four additional hours were expended in Johnson's preparations and execution of the Confederate advance, with Minty's troopers and artillery contesting the approach while falling back.

Johnson's lead infantry advanced in double-quick time as they neared the bridge and forced the Union troopers to retreat back over it in haste. A few planks of the flooring had been torn loose, without disabling the structure, before Johnson's infantry arrived. Minty accelerated the withdrawal under heavy fire when news arrived of Forrest's Confederate cavalry crossing at a nearby upstream ford. It was near the hour of 3:00 P.M. when Bushrod Johnson's division, followed by the vanguard of Longstreet's corps, under the command of Major General John Bell Hood, began crossing Chickamauga Creek via Reed's Bridge. By orders of Bragg, Hood took command of the column; accompanied by Forrest's cavalry, Hood led the force south toward the sound of fighting near Alexander's Bridge.[1]

DIRECTIONS: From the Visitor Center, turn left onto the LaFayette Road, right at the stoplight onto Reed's Bridge Road, and continue approximately 2.5 miles to the (unmarked) site of the bridge over Chickamauga Creek, located outside of the park boundaries. The site is not readily accessible to visitors for purposes other than crossing, although the road continues across the contested approach route of Johnson's infantry and over Pea Vine Ridge into Ringgold (six miles).

Reed's Bridge

This photograph (ca. 1895) of Reed's Bridge over Chickamauga Creek is a view from the north, downstream side. The appearance of the bridge is basically unchanged from Minty's description of "a narrow, frail structure, which was planked with loose boards and fence rails."[2] Reed's Bridge was partially dismantled by Minty's cavalry in the approach of Bushrod Johnson's infantry on September 18 and set ablaze by soldiers under the temporary command of Colonel Daniel McCook's infantry brigade of Granger's corps at daybreak of the nineteenth.

Waud's Sketch of Reed's Bridge

Artist Alfred R. Waud portrayed the climactic moment of Minty's collapsing defense of the vital bridge crossing when Confederate soldiers of Bushrod Johnson's division rushed forward to drive the Union cavalry troopers back before they could destroy the rickety structure.

Modern View of Reed's Bridge

A modern steel and concrete structure spans Chickamauga Creek at the site of the old Reed's Bridge outside of the park boundaries. To gain a perspective of the ground so heavily contested in the prelude to battle on September 18, 1863, visitors can follow the road crossing over the creek east along the line of approach from Pea Vine Ridge of the vanguard of Bragg's army. Foundation stones of the earlier wooden bridge are visible in the left foreground of this view from the north, just downstream of the bridge.

Open Grounds near Jay's Mill

Near the northeast boundary of the park, monuments at the intersection of Reed's Bridge and Jay's Mill roads commemorate the defense of Reed's Bridge on September 18 by units of Minty's Union cavalry brigade. This view of the Fourth Michigan Cavalry regimental monument, facing west across the expanded open fields of the postwar Reed farm, reveals part of the grounds where Colonel George G. Dibrell's dismounted cavalry and Brigadier General Matthew D. Ector's infantry advanced from the right of Forrest's line at Jay's Mill to the high ground defended by Van Derveer's Union infantry on the morning of September 19.

Alexander's Bridge

Another of the principal crossings of Chickamauga Creek, at Alexander's Bridge, created more delays for Confederate forces attempting to concentrate west of the creek above Lee and Gordon's Mill. Major General William H. T. Walker's Confederate reserve corps of two infantry divisions first approached Alexander's Bridge at the hour of 1:30 P.M., with Brigadier General St. John Liddell's division in the vanguard. Liddell ordered his lead brigade, under the command of Brigadier General Edward Walthall, to force the bridge crossing.

On the opposite creek bank, parts of three regiments of Colonel John T. Wilder's mounted infantry brigade were on hand to defend the critical bridge crossing. Armed with seven-shot Spencer repeating rifles and backed by the highly effective artillery support of a section of Captain Eli Lilly's Eighteenth Indiana Battery, these units fought dismounted from the cover of dense creekside thickets. Posted on a slight rise of ground several hundred yards to the rear of the front lines, Lilly's artillery enjoyed a clear field of fire over the then open fields of the Alexander farm grounds. In contrast, through an area of tangled woods and open fields east of the bridge, in narrow approaches defined by the twists and turns of the creek, Walthall managed to deploy no more than three of his five regiments to the front. Pinned down by the unusually heavy fire of the Spencer repeaters from the concealed Union lines, only one Confederate regiment, the Twenty-ninth Mississippi, advanced to the bridgehead.

After nearly three hours of fighting, both sides began to withdraw. The threat-ening advance of Bushrod Johnson's division and Nathan Bedford Forrest's cavalry from the vicinity of Reed's Bridge forced Wilder into a fighting withdrawal to the west, to the vicinity of the Viniard farm. When frontline Confederate troops reported that Wilder's troops had "torn up" the bridge, a condition masked during the earlier fighting by heavy undergrowth near the south bank, Walker directed his troops to march north to Lambert's ford, crossing Chickamauga Creek unopposed a mile north of Alexander's Bridge.[1] Despite the damage, Brigadier General Joseph Kershaw of Longstreet's command, arriving at the bridge crossing with his division late on the following day, reported that: "We moved . . . across Alexander's Bridge, over Chickamauga, and bivouacked at 1 A.M. on the 20th."[2]

DIRECTIONS: From the Visitor Center, drive south on the LaFayette Road approximately 2.75 miles. Turn left at the site of the Viniard farm onto Viniard-Alexander Road and continue 2.5 miles, turning right at the road junction to the designated park pull-off just before the yellow-painted bridge. Alternatively, from the site of Reed's Bridge, return west to the southeast park entrance at Jay's Mill Road, continue south on Jay's Mill Road, and bear to the left at the junction with the Alexander's Bridge Road, until the park pull-off just before the bridge.

Alexander's Bridge

The rustic appearance of postwar Alexander's Bridge is shown from a downstream view in this photograph (ca. 1890). After nearly four hours of stout defense by Wilder's brigade in the fighting on September 18, 1863, Confederate forces reached the creek bank where heavy undergrowth concealed the heavy damage Union work crews had inflicted on the structure and were redirected to an alternative, unopposed crossing one mile downstream.

Modern View of Alexander's Bridge

A steel bridge spans Chickamauga Creek in this present-day photograph of Alexander's Bridge from the east, looking upstream. Although the grounds to the immediate north (right) of the bridge were mostly open and cultivated field in 1863, in contrast to the heavy woodland now found there, trees and undergrowth along the creek banks reflect the general appearance reported by soldiers of Wilder's command, whose horses were "secured in the thicket below the bridge"[3] during the fighting with Walthall's Confederate brigade on September 18. Stone regimental markers identifying forward fighting positions of Wilder's command are located, out of view in this photograph, on the north side of the creek, on the lower grounds east and west of the bridge crossing.

Site of Eli Lilly's Artillery near Alexander's Bridge

Captain Eli Lilly of Wilder's brigade posted four rifled cannon of his artillery battery on this rise of ground some five hundred yards north of Alexander's Bridge. The guns were mounted in a grove of trees adjacent to a log cabin on the Alexander farmstead, with a clear field-of-fire to the south over open fields, firing canister and shell at a range of six hundred to twelve hundred yards. It was at the site of this battery during the fighting that a Confederate shell landed with a sputtering fuse. Private Sidney Speed was later commended by Lilly in recognition of his bravery when "seeing the fuse still burning, [he] picked it up from among my cannoneers and threw it over the house near by before it burst."[4]

McDonald Farm—Later Site of Visitor Center

The grounds of the McDonald farm remained the focus of strategy through-out the two days of battle. Located just south of the intersection of the Rossville-LaFayette stage road and a trail leading to McFarland's Gap Road, the farm-house stood on high ground at the crossroads of the principal two avenues of approach, or retreat, to Chattanooga. On September 8, when Bragg's army evac-uated the city eight miles north, long columns of Confederate infantry passed by the local farm fields in the withdrawal to the vicinity of LaFayette. Colonel Charles Harker's infantry brigade of Major General Thomas L. Crittenden's XXI Corps led the advance of Union units pursuing Bragg's army down the same route on the following day. Crittenden consolidated his forces in the vi-cinity of Lee and Gordon's Mill on Chickamauga Creek as the rest of the Union army moved south from the distant west, along two different routes leading to gaps through Lookout Mountain. After nine days of maneuvering by both armies far to the south, Major General George Thomas's XIV Infantry Corps led the Union army advance, hurrying to converge back north. Thomas arrived with leading elements of his corps in the early morning hours of September 19, bivouacking his tired soldiers at the Kelly farm, less than a mile south of McDonald's.

In the opening phase of battle, Colonel Ferdinand Van Derveer's Third Brigade of Brigadier General John M. Brannan's Third Division marched north from Kelly field and turned east in front of the McDonald house, cautiously following the route of a farm lane beginning directly opposite the house that eventually converged with Reed's Bridge Road.[1] Throughout the day, McDon-ald's open fields principally served as a staging ground for various Union units moving to attack in the forest to the east, and also as a site of regrouping for units retiring or driven from the fighting.[2] On the following morning, the Union army command would be slow in fortifying the McDonald farm position, and the oversight would have enormous repercussions.

DIRECTIONS: From I-24, Chattanooga, exit onto U.S. 27 south (sign for Chick-amauga Battlefield) and continue several miles to the posted park entrance. The Visitor Center is located on the right, just past the stoplight intersection of Reed's Bridge Road. From I-75 in north Georgia, exit west onto the Battle-field Parkway, continue to the intersection of U.S. 27 south, turn left, and pro-ceed to the park entrance.

Aerial View over Fields of McDonald Farm

This aerial photograph of the northern end of Chickamauga Battlefield Park, viewing northwest, includes distant glimpses of McFarland's Gap in Missionary Ridge (left background) and more distant Lookout Mountain. The Visitor Center (the first structure seen at the lower far right of this view) stands in a grove of trees on the elevated grounds of the McDonald farm, at the former site of the McDonald house. Just to the southeast, in the nearer cleared field, the white cupola of the Florida monument can be seen on the east side of the former route of the Rossville-LaFayette stage road that became the approximate dividing line between the opposing armies during the battle of Chickamauga. Directly across the road, four cannon in a grove of trees mark the elevated position of a Confederate artillery battery that supported Major General John C. Breckinridge's attack on September 20. Heavy regrowth of forest to the west of the cleared field behind the Visitor Center obscures the once open fields of the McDonald and Mullis farms that Major General Gordon Granger's reserve infantry traversed in the approach to Snodgrass Hill at a climactic moment in the battle. A part of the parade grounds of historic Fort Oglethorpe can be seen to the right of the Visitor Center.

1935 view

Modern view

Visitor/Administration Center near Site of McDonald House

Following the transfer of the National Military Park from the jurisdiction of the War Department to the National Park Service in 1933, the Georgian-style Administration Center for Chickamauga Battlefield (above left) was erected on the commanding high ground near the site of the McDonald house. By 1940, a columned front portico (above right) had been added to what became known as the Visitor Center. Newer facilities, including a modern multimedia complex, were constructed in 1989–90.

Most of the monuments and markers in the immediate vicinity relate to events of the second day of battle. At the crossroads where the LaFayette Road intersects Reed's Bridge Road, the Eighty-eighth Indiana regimental monument stands forward of the high ground defended during the advance of Brigadier General Daniel Adams's brigade of Breckinridge's division from the east. To the east, across the highway, the Forty-second Indiana monument stands at a position where that regiment fought in support on the right of the Eighty-eighth. Park position tablets on both sides of the highway and a battery of cannon on the north side of the buildings mark and describe the advance of Brigadier General St. John Liddell's division into the McDonald fields in the late afternoon of the twentieth and their retreat following the unexpected charge of Brigadier General John Turchin's brigade. A small metal plaque at the roadside in front of the Visitor Center, long since removed, marked the actual site of the McDonald house.

McCook's Position on Reed's Bridge Road

On the eve of battle, the armies converged to an inevitable collision south of Chattanooga. Rosecrans's delayed response to growing Confederate threats of envelopment of his dispersed army resulted in long columns of his infantry marching throughout the day and night in the mountainous north Georgia terrain from the southwest. Major General Thomas L. Crittenden's XXI Corps remained near the designated point of concentration at Lee and Gordon's Mill, while three infantry brigades of Major General Gordon Granger's reserve corps were stationed along the line of Missionary Ridge, to the north, near Rossville. Union cavalry units and Colonel John T. Wilder's mounted infantry brigade, on detached service, fought hard throughout much of the day to block advance Confederate forces approaching Chickamauga Creek from the east and south. Granger dispatched two infantry brigades from Rossville to reinforce Colonel Robert Minty's cavalry at Reed's Bridge. Granger's lead brigade, under the command of Colonel Daniel McCook, arrived at the scene too late, in the early evening. Minty's cavalry had already withdrawn from Reed's Bridge, along with Wilder's force at Alexander's Bridge. Confederate General John Bell Hood's column of three advance brigades of Longstreet's corps and Brigadier General Bushrod Johnson's division, delayed several hours in forcing the passage at Reed's Bridge, turned south after crossing and joined forces with Major General William H. T. Walker's reserve corps near Alexander's Bridge. McCook's Union brigade deployed on a low ridge astride Reed's Bridge Road, several hundred yards west of the bridge, with Colonel John Mitchell's brigade posted to the rear. In what would prove to be a significant miscalculation, McCook

interviewed several Confederate prisoners captured from straggling elements of Bushrod Johnson's division and concluded that only a single enemy brigade had crossed Reed's Bridge.

At daylight on the nineteenth, a detachment of McCook's command moved down to Chickamauga Creek with orders to destroy Reed's Bridge with burning fence rails.[1] Reconnaissance units of Brigadier General Henry Davidson's brigade of Brigadier General Nathan Bedford Forrest's cavalry observed the activity as they approached and charged from the south before the bridge could be destroyed. Another small Union detachment filling canteens from a small stream near Jay's Mill also fled from the charge of the Confederate troopers.[2] At the hour of 7:00 A.M., with Confederate cavalry in pursuit of the scattered detachments, McCook's and Mitchell's brigades were withdrawing west, under fire, with new orders to rejoin Granger. Two infantry brigades of Major General George Thomas's lead division were coming down from the LaFayette Road to investigate and, possibly, capture the lone Confederate brigade McCook had reported.[3]

DIRECTIONS: From the Visitor Center, exit left to the stoplight intersection, turn right onto Reed's Bridge Road, and proceed approximately two miles to the pull-off with three monuments on the right and three monuments, with two cannon, on the left. Along the way are the sites of the Tennessee Artillery Monument and Colonel Ferdinand Van Derveer's position.

Portion of Battlefield East of the Visitor Center

Dense forest covers much of the battlefield to the east of the LaFayette Road. In this 1985 aerial photograph, looking southeast, the view encompasses most of the area of heavy fighting through the morning hours of September 19. The outline of Reed's Bridge Road can be traced near the left border of the wooded terrain, angling sharply to the right near far left center. Dan McCook's position along Reed's Bridge Road, just to the northwest of the site of Jay's Mill, is located near the eastern park boundary, marked by the upper, angled border of the forest, where the faint outline of Reed's Bridge Road can be seen intersecting that boundary at upper left. The large cleared area at the upper right of center is Winfrey field. Despite the daunting appearance of the dense forest canopy, roads and more than thirty-five miles of hiking and horse trails provide access to nearly all of the hidden monuments, markers, and lines of battle.

McCook's Position on Reed's Bridge Road

Monuments and markers stand in a small clearing along Reed's Bridge Road approximately three hundred yards from the intersection with Jay's Mill Road, at a site with only a very small combat role in the battle. This is where the commanding officer on the scene, Colonel Daniel McCook of Granger's reserve corps, found evidence of what he believed was a stranded Confederate brigade near Reed's Bridge and later reported to Major General George Thomas, setting in motion Thomas's seizing of the initiative by the advance of Brannan's division.

McCook's Position on Reed's Bridge Road—Sixty-ninth Ohio Monument

Daniel McCook's brigade of Granger's reserve corps arrived at the high ground some four hundred yards northeast of Jay's Mill in the early evening of September 18, with Colonel John Mitchell's brigade posted a short distance to the west. The regimental monument in this photograph (ca. 1896), viewing southwest, stands where the Sixty-ninth Ohio, temporarily assigned to McCook's command, left camp in the pre-dawn darkness of September 19 with instructions to complete the destruction of nearby Reed's Bridge. In action later reported by Dan McCook and portrayed in the bas-relief sculpture on the monument, the Ohio soldiers "gallantly charged across the bridge, drove the enemy from it, and set it on fire."[4] Extensive postwar clearing in the vicinity of Jay's Mill opened the woods where McCook's command bivouacked, exposing part of the approaches to Colonel Ferdinand Van Derveer's position in the left background of this view across Reed's Bridge Road.

Jay's Mill—Opening of the Battle

At daylight, Bragg ordered Brigadier General Nathan Bedford Forrest's cavalry to ride north along the route of Jay's Mill Road to reconnoiter and provide a screen for the gathering Confederate forces west of Chickamauga Creek. Forrest departed with Brigadier General Henry Davidson's cavalry brigade at a time when no one in the Confederate ranks knew, or reported, that advance Union troops of Thomas's XIV Corps were bivouacked in Kelly field, at a distance of less than one half mile from the right front units of the Confederate army.

In response to Colonel Daniel McCook's report of an isolated Confederate brigade near Reed's Bridge, Thomas ordered units of Brannan's division to reconnoiter to the east and capture the alleged stranded enemy force west of Chickamauga Creek.[1] By the hour of 7:30 A.M., Bragg's army stood poised to attack from both sides of Chickamauga Creek in the vicinity of Lee and Gordon's Mill when unexpected heavy gunfire erupted to the north. Brannan's lead infantry brigade, under the command of Colonel John Croxton, had opened fire on an advance patrol of Forrest's cavalry after moving forward approximately one mile from Kelly field. Croxton's line of skirmishers, moving through heavy woods west of the site of Jay's Mill, were driven back by a reckless charge of the Tenth Confederate Cavalry before volleys of musket fire revealed the unseen front line of Union infantry. Surviving Confederates raced back in shock through the lines of Davidson's brigade of Brigadier General John Pegram's division, Forrest's cavalry, resting from their recent pursuit of McCook's and Colonel John Mitchell's brigades. Pegram and Forrest scrambled to form a line of battle in thick woods crowning the first ridge above the open grounds of the sawmill. Forrest immediately sent a courier to headquarters for the release of his other cavalry units, then ordering Pegram to hold his position with Davidson's lone brigade until reinforcements arrived, he galloped south to find available infantry units.

For more than an hour, Davidson's brigade of cavalry, fighting dismounted from the cover of a bordering rail fence, trees, and stumps, struggled alone, retreating and re-advancing, to hold back the five infantry regiments of Croxton's brigade. In this fight, before support arrived, Davidson lost more than a quarter of the men under his command.[2] Forrest raced back to coordinate the fighting, with news of significant incoming support. Bragg had responded to his urgent request for infantry support by ordering the dispatch of one the closest units: Colonel Claudius Wilson's brigade of Brigadier General States Rights Gist's division, Major General H. T. Walker's reserve corps. Additional cavalry support arrived first. Croxton's advance temporarily stalled, and troops were shifted to his left when Colonel George Dibrell's Confederate cavalry brigade arrived from the south and moved up, dismounted, on the right of Davidson's line of battle.[3]

Infantry forces from both armies were nearing the scene. The battle that opened in deep woods near a frontier sawmill, at a time and place neither army commander expected, would expand in scope throughout the day as successive fresh units were rushed to the widening front.

DIRECTIONS: From the Visitor Center, exit left to the stoplight intersection, turn right onto Reed's Bridge Road, and proceed 2.2 miles to the junction of Jay's Mill Road. Turn right and proceed approximately 0.1 mile to the pull-off for the site of Jay's Mill.

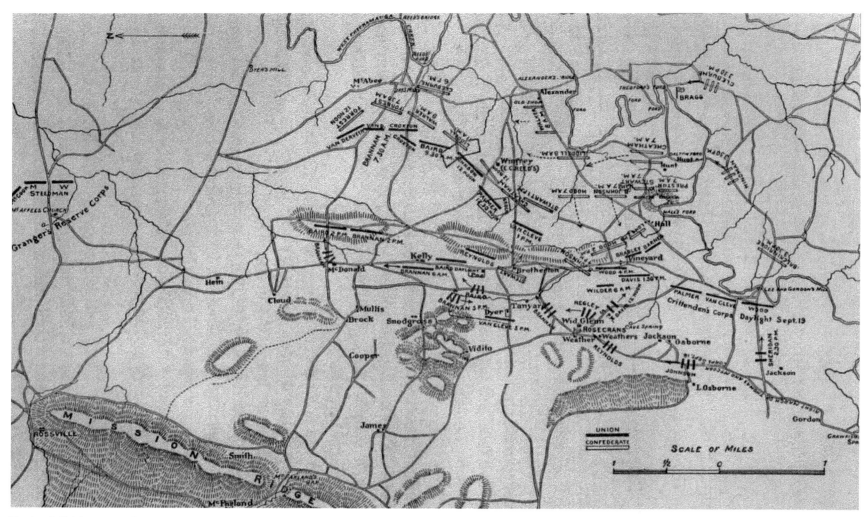

Battle of Chickamauga, September 19, 1863

Site of Jay's Mill

This photograph (ca. 1895) provides a postwar perspective to the northwest of the open grounds extending from the site of Jay's Mill. The open grounds are more extensive than the armies found in 1863, when the fields were bordered by woods to the west as close as the large cedar tree in the center of this postwar view.[4] Croxton's brigade of Brannan's division approached from the west to within several hundred yards of the trees to the far left of this view. Davidson's brigade of Forrest's cavalry fought, dismounted, along the line of the rail fence on the first low ridge to the west. A small park fingerpost to the left of this view points to the actual site of the steam sawmill. The location of the spring, the source of water sought by Dan McCook's early morning patrol, is noted by the "loose pile of stones in front of the fence"[5] in the center foreground of this image. Near the site of the sawmill, cavalry and infantry reinforcements sent to Forrest advanced to the front along the northwest line of this spring. Van Derveer's brigade fought on the high ground in wooded terrain to the distant northwest (left of center in this view). The small image of a postwar house can be seen on the far right, along the route of Reed's Bridge Road.[6]

Modern View of Jay's Mill Site

In 1863, the open grounds at Jay's Mill extended north (to the right of this modern view) to Reed's Bridge Road, as now, and nearly two hundred yards to the west up the slope of rising ground. Davidson's brigade of Forrest's cavalry fought along the crest of the first low ridge to the west, in wooded terrain just beyond the boundary of a smaller, cultivated field. Forward positions of Union infantry units of Croxton's brigade are marked by monuments on the crest of the second ridge to the west, approximately 250 yards farther west from the Confederate position.

A red-lettered park tablet, just visible at the tree line in the left-of-center background, marks a location where Captain Gustave Huwald's Tennessee battery opened fire on retiring units of Dan McCook's brigade prior to the arrival of Croxton's brigade. The small fingerpost pointing to the site of the steam sawmill stands by the paved roadside of modern Jay's Mill Road, at the lower right of this present-day photograph. In this view, the site of the mill lies at the base of the small cedar trees to the extreme left, beside the millstream. At the far right of this view, the grouping of monuments commemorating Minty's defense of Reed's Bridge can be glimpsed at the intersection of Reed's Bridge Road.

Plat of Fields at Jay's Mill

Steam-Driven Sawmill on Lookout Mountain

This historical image (ca. 1865) attributed to the Mathew Brady Studios, under the direction of the War Department, Office of the Chief Signal Officer, shows a steam-driven sawmill in operation on Lookout Mountain, Tennessee. No images have been found to compare how much the small, improvised, portable steam-driven sawmill near Reed's Bridge resembled this federal government facility on Lookout Mountain. The small millstream at the site of Jay's Mill represents the prime site prerequisite for any such steam-driven engine: water. It was this water that drew a thirsty detachment of Union soldiers from Daniel McCook's brigade, in the early morning hours of September 19, and first attracted the attention of advance units of Forrest's Confederate cavalry.

Portable Steam-Driven Sawmill

The wagon-portable steam-driven saw at Jay's Mill may have looked similar to this one, photographed in operation at an Arkansas farm in the early 1900s. Beginning in the mid-nineteenth century, portable steam sawmills helped considerably in opening frontier settlements, such as the one in West Chickamauga Valley near Reed's Bridge. Operators of these belt-driven machines would move on when the available supply of timber or demand was exhausted. Such mills were utilized through the early years of the twentieth century, until more efficient gasoline engines displaced most of the steam models.

Vicinity of Wilson's Attack

The battle opened by Forrest's cavalry and Croxton's brigade of Brannan's division near the site of Jay's Mill intensified as reinforcements from both sides were hurried to the front. At a time when Dibrell's dismounted cavalry brigade fought with Ferdinand Van Derveer's infantry brigade on Forrest's right, and Davidson's dismounted cavalry struggled to hold on at Jay's Mill, Wilson's infantry brigade of Gist's Confederate reserve division crossed the Brotherton Road from the south in line of battle and struck Croxton's right flank. Wilson's determined attack forced Croxton to fall back several hundred yards and redeploy his brigade facing south.[1]

As Dibrell's frontal attack on Van Derveer's position faltered, Forrest himself brought up Brigadier General Matthew Ector's infantry brigade of Gist's division to continue the pressure. In a later, facetious report to Thomas, after battling four or five infantry brigades instead of the single stranded unit he had been ordered to capture, Colonel Croxton supposedly remarked: "General, I would have brought them to you if I had known which ones you wanted!"[2]

Brannan forwarded part of the First Brigade, Colonel John Connell's command, to reinforce both Croxton and Van Derveer. Thomas reacted to the threat of the growing Confederate force by next dispatching Brigadier General Absalom Baird's First Division. The arrival of Brigadier General John King's Third Brigade of U.S. regular infantry allowed Croxton to withdraw and replenish ammunition. Baird's next brigade to arrive, under the command of Colonel Benjamin Scribner, struck hard on the left flank of Wilson's line of battle near the Winfrey field and drove the Confederates back with heavy losses. Wilson's attack ended in a disorderly retreat, and Davidson's cavalry again fell back to the vicinity of Jay's Mill. Scribner failed to press his advantage, deploying his brigade along the upper, north end of Winfrey field.[3] A brief lull in the fighting ensued as both sides regrouped and rested in the smoke-filled forest. Nearly all of the fighting had taken place within a widening area of dense forest between the Brotherton and Reed's Bridge roads, where limited visibility increased the odds of surprise in flanking attacks. More than three hours had elapsed since the opening of the battle, and the heaviest fighting had yet to begin. Heavy columns of fresh Confederate and Union infantry were approaching the scene from the south and from the west.[4]

DIRECTIONS: From the site of Jay's Mill, turn right at the adjacent junction of the Brotherton Road, proceed 0.3 mile and park on the left at the site of Bragg's September 20 headquarters.

A. R. Waud, Hulton Archive/Getty Images

Site of General Braxton Bragg's Headquarters on the Brotherton Road

Thick forest surrounds the shell monument marking the site of Bragg's headquarters on the afternoon of the second day of battle. The soldiers who fought in this locale found varying conditions, with some areas, by the report of Major General George Thomas, "interspersed with undergrowth . . . so dense it is difficult to see fifty paces ahead."[5] A few cleared fields, often under cultivation, were scattered through the woods while other areas of the forest were relatively free of troublesome undergrowth. Gunfire exchanges at ranges up to three hundred yards were reported.[6] Small stone monuments marking the advance of Georgia infantry are located at the north end of the trail leading to this site. These units of Wilson's brigade comprised part of the first infantry reinforcements for General Forrest at Jay's Mill; Wilson's regiments advanced across the Brotherton Road on a broad front to strike the right flank of Croxton's line of battle formed in the woods ahead.

Longstreet's Arrival at Bragg's Headquarters

This drawing by noted sketch artist Alfred R. Waud depicts the scene at Bragg's headquarters, then located near the Thedford Ford crossing of Chickamauga Creek, when Lieutenant General James Longstreet arrived in the late evening hours of September 19. There is tension depicted in the two figures, as Bragg is awakened. In the midst of a great battle, Bragg had failed to send an escort to Longstreet upon his arrival by train at Catoosa Station, near Ringgold. Longstreet had nearly been captured as he and his staff approached a Union outpost in darkness, searching for the approach to Bragg's army. In the conference between the two that followed, Bragg informed Longstreet of his newly formed left wing command and outlined the battle plans for the next day. There is a possible discrepancy in this depiction; reports say that an ailing Bragg at this time slept in an army ambulance wagon rather than a tent.[7] Bragg's headquarters was moved to the location near the Brotherton Road on September 20.

Winfrey Field

As successive Union infantry units arrived from the south, each was quickly dispatched to support Thomas's hard-pressed forces in the forest east of the LaFayette Road. In the ongoing race of both armies to the battle zone, Walker's other Confederate reserve corps division, under the command of Brigadier General St. John Liddell, arrived next. Taking advantage of a lull in the fighting after Absalom Baird's rout of Wilson's brigade, Liddell carefully arranged a line of battle in the cover of woods in front of the Winfrey house on the Alexander's Bridge Road.

Some time past the hour of 11:00 A.M., Liddell's forces advanced to the attack, with Colonel Daniel Govan's brigade on the left and Brigadier General Edward Walthall's on the right. Some five hundred yards to the north, Baird's three infantry brigades rested in positions facing east, all in the vicinity of the Winfrey cornfield, separated from each other by several hundred yards. Colonel Benjamin Scribner's brigade had been posted on the north end of the open field, supported by Lieutenant George Van Pelt's artillery battery. Brigadier General John Starkweather's brigade had been deployed in reserve, on a nearby ridge to the northwest, while Brigadier General John King's brigade of U.S. regular infantry lay several hundred yards northeast, on the ridge formerly occupied by Croxton.

Liddell's attack caught the Union units by surprise. With Govan's brigade breaking through Scribner's right flank, Walthall's brigade swept through the open Winfrey field from the southwest, overwhelming Scribner's line of battle at the north end and continuing through the woods to overrun King's brigade. Govan's brigade had continued success attacking through the woods west of the open field, leading to the rout of Starkweather's reserve brigade.

Many of the surviving Union soldiers ran from the scene, some stopping only after they reached the LaFayette Road.[1] Three batteries of Union artillery were captured or disabled, including Van Pelt's First Michigan of Scribner's. Nearly all of the lost guns were subsequently recaptured when Liddell's attack collapsed in the approach to Van Derveer's reinforced line of battle near Reed's Bridge Road.[2] Liddell's retreat accelerated as Croxton's brigade returned to strike the Confederate left flank. Liddell led his division back to the original lines near the Winfrey house.

The sloping terrain of the open Winfrey field and aggressive tactics contributed to Liddell's initial success. Although Van Pelt's artillery battery fired a total of sixty-four rounds of canister into the Confederates' approach, Scribner's infantry in front were able to fire effectively only at short range.[3]

A later attack by Liddell in support of Major General Benjamin Cheatham's division brought Walthall's brigade, crossing Winfrey field from the east, up against the Union units of Brigadier General Richard Johnson's division aligned along the opposite, west border of the open field. This attack collapsed under heavy musket and artillery fire within fifteen minutes.[4] A final Confederate assault through Winfrey field would be launched in the closing minutes of daylight by units of Major General Patrick Cleburne's division, a confused sound-and-light spectacle in near total darkness that would end the fighting on the first day of battle.

DIRECTIONS: From the site of Bragg's Headquarters, proceed west on the Brotherton Road 0.3 mile to the east border of the open Winfrey field and continue west to the opposite border of the field. Park in the space provided near the sign for the Baldwin monument.

Aerial View of Winfrey Field

Winfrey Field is an isolated clearing in the densely wooded battlefield east of the LaFayette Road, slightly more than a hundred yards southwest of the intersection with the Alexander's Bridge Road. In this aerial photograph, viewing southeast, the Brotherton Road can be seen crossing the field where two cannon, barely visible midway across, represent two Confederate batteries at their closest approach to the Union lines during Cleburne's early evening attack. The white object at the tree line, lower center, is the Ninety-third Ohio monument, commemorating a unit posted near the left flank of Colonel Philemon Baldwin's line of defense along the upper end of Winfrey field at the time of Cleburne's assault. The shell monument marking the site where Baldwin was mortally wounded is hidden beneath the trees at the lower right of the field.

Artillery at the Front of Cleburne's Night Attack in Winfrey Field

Four separate Confederate assaults swept across Winfrey Field on the first day of battle. These included Wilson's left flank advance in the early morning attack on Croxton's brigade, two separate charges of Walthall's brigade, Liddell's division, and the final twilight charge of the center of Cleburne's division. The two cannon in the foreground mark the closest approach of Calvert's and Semple's artillery during Cleburne's night attack. A short section of rail fence located in the left background is a reconstruction representing the boundary fence of Winfrey field at the time of the battle. Union troops added rocks and broken tree limbs to fortify their position at the upper end of the field in the afternoon. A tall shell monument at the far left corner of the field, masked by the high grass in this view, marks the site where Baldwin was mortally wounded, shot from his horse while attempting to lead a counter-charge of his Union infantry brigade at the time of Cleburne's attack.

Lieutenant Van Pelt Defends His Battery

This steel engraving of a Thomas Nast painting is a stylized depiction of Lieutenant George Van Pelt defending the guns of his Michigan battery at Winfrey field. In the climactic moment of confrontation with the onrushing Confederates of Liddell's division, his infantry support driven from the field, Van Pelt was killed after drawing his sword in a last act of defiance. Five other men of the gunnery crews were killed, seven seriously wounded, thirteen captured, and five of the six ten-pounder Parrott guns in the battery were captured.[5] All of the guns were later reported recaptured.

Site of Lieutenant Van Pelt's Battery — North Winfrey Field

A glimpse of upper Winfrey field is visible through the trees from this monument at the site of Loomis's Battery A, First Michigan Artillery. This veteran battery of six rifled Parrott guns, commanded at Chickamauga by Van Pelt, was overrun by the two Confederate brigades of Liddell's division in the late morning attack enveloping Winfrey field. The high ground of the upper Winfrey field provided little advantage to Union infantry posted in front of the guns, as the Confederates launched enveloping flank attacks from the wooded areas east and west and Walthall's men charged aggressively from the cover of the depression in the open ground near the line of the Brotherton Road.[6] A small inscribed block of stone a few steps forward of the site of the battery marks the line of battle of Scribner's Union infantry at the present tree line. At the time of Liddell's attack, Van Pelt's guns were aimed to fire in a southwest direction, to the right of this view, in response to the approaching Confederate infantry initially concealed in the wooded low ground with heavy undergrowth beyond the open field.

Van Derveer's Position on Reed's Bridge Road

In the opening phase of battle, Colonel Ferdinand Van Derveer's Union brigade moved east from the McDonald farm along the route of a trail leading to Reed's Bridge Road. The advance was halted within a mile to the east at the crest of a rise approximately one mile northeast of Jay's Mill. At a time when Colonel John Croxton was heavily engaged on his far right, Van Derveer selected a naturally strong defensive position with commanding slopes in front and to the north.[1] Two regiments and a battery of artillery had just been deployed forward on the lower slopes in front when the dismounted Confederate cavalry of Colonel George Dibrell's brigade approached. After several strongly pressed and costly attempts failed to even reach Van Derveer's front line, Dibrell ordered a withdrawal, just as Brigadier General Matthew Ector's Confederate infantry brigade began moving up in support. Ector's slightly mistimed advance through Dibrell's line of retreat suffered the same end result in the face of Van Derveer's well-positioned and effectively coordinated defense.

When subsequent Union reinforcements (Brigadier General Absalom Baird's division) broke in the spectacular advance of Liddell's Confederate division from the south, Van Derveer's recently reinforced infantry and artillery held their fire as stampeded Union soldiers ran through their lines, then brought the Confederate advance to a halt with concentrated volleys of musket fire and canister. Liddell's winded troops retreated in reaction to an unauthorized and aggressive countercharge by the Ninth Ohio regiment, at a time when Van Derveer's fourth and final challenge of the day neared the north slopes behind his lines. Brigadier General Nathan Bedford Forrest had dispatched Dibrell's dismounted cavalry across Reed's Bridge Road and up through the dense woods north of the Union lines. Racing to reposition his infantry and artillery in the opposite direction on the crest of the high ground across Reed's Bridge Road, where Dibrell's front line approached from below, Van Derveer succeeded in forming a line of battle with converging angles of fire. Heavy casualties were inflicted in the ranks of the advancing Confederates, who approached within forty yards of the upper Union lines before conceding defeat in what Van Derveer later described as a "sullen withdrawal."

Within a span of four hours through the morning, the troops of Van Derveer's brigade had successfully stood their ground in four different engagements with Confederate units incoming from three directions at four separate intervals of time. By late afternoon, with no further action from Confederate forces on his front, Van Derveer withdrew his brigade under orders to consolidate with Brigadier General John M. Brannan's division near the Kelly farm.[2]

DIRECTIONS: The pull-off on Reed's Bridge Road for the cannon and markers at the site of Van Derveer's position is located one mile east of the intersection with the LaFayette Road, en route to the previously mentioned site of McCook's brigade.

Van Derveer's Position on Reed's Bridge Road

Van Derveer's Union infantry brigade of Brannan's division occupied this commanding position, slightly less than a mile northwest of Jay's Mill, during the opening of the battle, with lines extending to the right through the woods in support of Croxton's brigade. A battery of artillery anchored this left flank position, while two of Van Derveer's regiments were sent down the wooded slopes in front. To the east, the ground slopes down—in a series of lower ridges—approximately eighty feet in elevation to the site of the mill. At the time of the battle, the woods in front were more open, enabling clear and destructive fire into the lines of advancing Confederates. The park tablet on the opposite side of the road marks the realignment of Van Derveer's men at the time of the flank attack of Dibrell's dismounted cavalry, where the ground slopes down in a northerly direction.

View from Reed's Bridge Tower

This photograph from the early 1900s provides a view to the west from the upper level of the Reed's Bridge (also called Baird's) observation tower erected at the time of the development of the battlefield park. The Reed's Bridge tower was erected on the original line of Van Derveer's brigade at the opening of the battle at a position just in rear of the infantry right flank.[3] In the far distance, beyond the heavily wooded terrain that shaped the nature of fighting on the morning of the first day of battle, beginning from the upper left of the photograph, the buildings and cleared fields of Fort Oglethorpe can be seen. In the words of one of the principal leaders of the development of the battlefield park, Henry Boynton, a colonel commanding the Thirty-fifth Ohio Regiment of Van Derveer's brigade: "The strategy of the campaigns and the movements of the battles are readily understood by the views afforded from . . . [the observation towers]."[4]

Preston Smith and Seventy-seventh Pennsylvania Monuments—Cleburne's Twilight Assault

In the closing hour of daylight, at 6:00 P.M., Major General Patrick Cleburne's division attacked Union forces remaining in the vicinity of Winfrey Field. The Confederate attack coincidentally began at a time when Thomas had ordered a withdrawal of these Union units to a new, consolidated line of battle at the Kelly farm.[1] Cleburne's line of battle stretched one mile in width, with Brigadier General Lucius Polk's brigade on the right at Jay's Mill, Brigadier General S. A. M. Wood's brigade in the center, below Winfrey Field, and Brigadier General James Deshler's brigade on the left, supported by two brigades of Benjamin Cheatham's division.[2]

Advancing through the darkening woodland, Lucius Polk's brigade encountered the reformed brigades of Colonel Benjamin Scribner and Brigadier General John Starkweather north of Winfrey Field. Lucius Polk attacked as the Union brigades became entangled and unintentionally fired into each other's own ranks. Once again, Scribner's and Starkweather's brigades were driven back in disarray.[3]

In the center of Cleburne's battle line, Wood's brigade had limited success in the night attack launched through Winfrey Field from the southeast. Cleburne later reported: "For half an hour the firing was the heaviest I had ever heard. . . . Each party was aiming at the flashes of the other guns, and few of the shot from either side took effect. . . . Captain [Henry] Semple and Lieutenant [Thomas] Key ran their batteries forward within 60 yards of the enemy's line and opened a rapid fire. [Lucius] Polk pressed forward at the same moment on the right, when the enemy ceased firing and quickly disappeared from my front."[4] Colonel Philemon P. Baldwin, commanding a brigade of Brigadier General Richard Johnson's Union division, was fatally shot in this attack on his position at the upper end of the open field.

On Cleburne's left, Deshler's brigade drifted out of position to the west, exposing Brigadier General Preston Smith's brigade moving up in support. Smith was shot and killed as he approached the line of the Seventy-seventh Pennsylvania Regiment on the assumption that the dimly seen soldiers in front were part of Deshler's line. In the immediate aftermath, the Union regiment was surrounded and captured intact, although many of the prisoners escaped by simply walking away in the darkness. Deshler's and Smith's advance then stalled in the utter confusion of the night fighting. All remaining Union units were quietly withdrawn to the new position at the Kelly farm as Cleburne's men bivouacked for the night where the fighting stopped.[5]

DIRECTIONS: From Winfrey Field, proceed west on the Brotherton Road to the nearby intersection with the Alexander's Bridge Road. Turn left, proceed approximately 0.1 mile, and park in the pull-off on the right. Follow the trail beginning near the park sign for the Smith monument to reach the site that also includes the Seventy-seventh Pennsylvania monument.

General Preston Smith and Seventy-seventh Pennsylvania Monuments

Brigadier General Preston Smith was mortally wounded in an eruption of gunfire from startled Union soldiers at the site where the pyramid monument now stands. The adjacent monument in the background stands on the line of battle of the Seventy-seventh Pennsylvania Regiment at the time General Smith approached, in the early afternoon of September 19. Brigadier General John K. Jackson's and Brigadier General George Maney's brigades of Cheatham's division advanced to the attack north of Brock field through this area in the afternoon fighting and retreated in haste along the same route. Colonel George Dibrell's brigade of Brigadier General Nathan Bedford Forrest's cavalry provided critical support that slowed the aggressive approach of Richard Johnson's Union infantry division. The Seventy-seventh Pennsylvania anchored the forward left flank of Colonel Joseph Dodge's Second Brigade of Richard Johnson's division on the elevated ground where the regimental monument now stands.

Survivors of Seventy-seventh Pennsylvania at Dedication of Battlefield Monument

Surviving veterans of the Seventy-seventh Pennsylvania Regiment pose at the dedication of their unit's monument on Chickamauga Battlefield, November 13, 1897. Prominent in the background, on the face of the monument, is a bronze bas-relief tablet depicting the night battle scene during the attacks of Deshler's and, subsequently, Smith's brigade, "at the time when General Smith and Staff rode into the line of the 77th Pennsylvania Infantry."[6] This photograph is a view from the southeast near the site of the Smith shell monument.

Brock Field

When Brigadier General St. John Liddell's morning attack collapsed, two fresh Union infantry divisions, comprising six brigades, were filing through the woods from the west on a wide front extending from the Kelly field to the Brotherton farm. On the left of this line of advance, Major General Richard Johnson's three brigades were moving "in the direction of the cannonading."[1] On the right, the three brigades of Major General John Palmer's division were nearing the open field of the Brock farm at nearly the same moment as the latest Confederate reinforcements.[2] Cheatham advanced his Confederate division on a three brigade front, with two in reserve, through the woods from the southeast. On Cheatham's right, Jackson's brigade first encountered Croxton's Union brigade and steadily drove it back to the west, reaching a low ridge just north of Brock field. There, Jackson halted in line of battle, while Croxton's infantry in their front passed through the lines of Richard Johnson's incoming division.[3]

On Jackson's left, Brigadier General William Hazen's brigade of Major General John Palmer's Union division arrived first in the open Brock field, fighting for position against Brigadier General Preston Smith's Confederate brigade approaching from the wooded east border. Palmer's other two brigades moved into supporting positions west of the open field, in dense woods where "few positions could be found for the effective use of artillery."[4] For nearly three hours, Smith's and Brigadier General Otho Strahl's brigades fought to a standstill with Hazen's and, later, Brigadier General John Turchin's brigades in Brock field. Units of three additional Union infantry divisions were dispatched to the area surrounding the Brock farm to contain Cheatham's powerful attack. Ammunition became a critical problem for both sides in the furious exchanges of musket fire, and brigades on both sides were withdrawn and replaced. Briga-

dier General George Maney's brigade replaced Jackson's brigade, on the low ridge just north of the open field. As Maney's ammunition dwindled, Richard Johnson launched a coordinated assault with his three brigades that accelerated Maney's withdrawal into a complete rout.

Cheatham's fifth infantry brigade, under the command of Brigadier General Marcus Wright, moved into position on the far left of Cheatham's broad front attack at the Brock farm and was immediately under fire at close quarters with the two right brigades of Palmer's division in an area of dense woods with entangling undergrowth. Wright's advance stalled, then collapsed into a rapid retreat as Brigadier General Sam Beatty's brigade of Brigadier General Horatio P. Van Cleve's Union infantry division charged in on the Confederate left flank, with only Captain William Carnes's Tennessee battery providing covering fire. Cheatham ended the struggle for Brock field in midafternoon with the withdrawal of his remaining brigades to the vicinity of the Winfrey house.[5]

DIRECTIONS: From the site of the pull-off on Alexander's Bridge Road, at the trail to the Smith monument, reverse direction and return to the intersection of the Brotherton Road. Turn left and proceed 0.3 mile to the designated parking area on the right at Brock field. The site of Carnes's battery can be approached by a horse and foot trail (watch for the distinctive park horse trail sign) that crosses the Brotherton Road approximately one half mile beyond (west of) Brock field. A monument flanked by cannon marks the site at the end of a short foot trail branching from the horse and foot trail at the position of a park tablet marking a position of Van Cleve's infantry division.

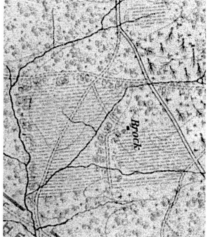

Plat of Fields at Brock Farm

Brock Field

The cleared fields of the John Brock farm were the scene of sustained close-range combat in the early afternoon of September 19. From the perspective of this photograph, viewing south from the Brotherton Road, Hazen's brigade of John Palmer's division advanced into the open field from the right, moving forward in an easterly direction to confront Confederate infantry from Smith's brigade emerging from the tree-lined border to the left. Part of Hazen's line of battle can be traced by the imaginary line between the two large monuments visible in the far distance, at the left and center of this view, marking forward positions of the 124th (left) and 41st Ohio (right) infantry regiments. Part of Hazen's artillery, Battery F, First Ohio Light, operated from the position marked by both the inscribed park tablet at left foreground of this view and the state of Ohio's small granite marker that is only partially visible directly behind the tablet. Brock field slopes downward near the tree-lined borders of this view, where a number of small stone markers for the forward positions of the Tennessee regiments of Smith's and Strahl's brigades are located.

The Brock fields at the time of the battle were much more extensive than found today. As the inset map, drawn by Edward E. Betts, park engineer, in 1896, shows (above right), substantially more acreage to the southwest had been cleared and was fought over. Wright's brigade advanced through and fought mostly in the tangled woods to the west, where Union reinforcements occupied a commanding ridge less than three hundred yards east of the Brotherton farm.

124th Regiment, Ohio Infantry, in Brock Field

This photograph of the 124th Ohio regimental monument in Brock field (ca. 1896) is a view from the east, the perspective of Smith's and, later, Strahl's right flank units of Confederate infantry as they approached the left center of Hazen's brigade at the time of battle. A line of trees in the background follows the west border of Brock field. The Brock house was located in the wooded area along the southwest border of the field, at the focus of a scene of more heavy fighting between Cheatham's left and the right two brigades of Palmer's division.

Maney's Position North of Brock Field

The park tablet in the foreground of this view from the northeast marks a forward position of Maney's brigade of Cheatham's division, at the upper north end of the "ridge well wooded," as described in Maney's post-action report. Defensively, the elevated position provided several hundred yards of "clear open woods"[6] to the front, sloping gradually to the west. That view is currently blocked by the regrowth of forest at the site. At the time of the battle, a large acreage of woodland north and northwest of Brock field had been substantially cleared, with a strip of newly felled timber across the ground of the lower Confederate approach route to the ridge.[7]

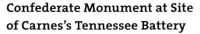
Above: Ca. 1900 view
Right: Modern view

Confederate Monument at Site of Carnes's Tennessee Battery

Captain William Carnes, desperate to move his artillery battery up with Wright's brigade of infantry on the left of Cheatham's broad frontal attack, detailed men with axes to cut through entangling undergrowth amid thick woods. Carnes's battery reached the front at a time when Wright's attack had stalled under the fire of Palmer's right echelon infantry, and retreat was immi-

nent as Union reinforcements of Van Cleve's division approached the Confederate left flank. Firing double charges of canister at close quarters, Carnes's battery succeeded in checking Union troops approaching in front until nearly surrounded by others closing in from the left and rear. With heavy troop casualties and only ten surviving horses of the battery's fifty-nine, Carnes ordered the remaining crew to evacuate. After firing a few more rounds, Carnes and a

gunnery sergeant mounted horses and raced back through the forest to rejoin their command. The four cannon of the battery were captured, then shortly thereafter recaptured by the advance of Major General Alexander P. Stewart's division. In this early park photograph (above left), open woods cleared of undergrowth surround the site, which is less than four hundred feet southeast of the elevated ridge where Union infantry of Van Cleve's division moved down in

the attack that captured Carnes's battery and accelerated Wright's withdrawal.[8]

In the modern photograph, bushes and small tree foliage surround the clearing for the Carnes battery monument and four cannon, in an area of generally open woods interspersed with patches of undergrowth that can be troublesome for those straying from the trail, though much less entangling than that encountered by Carnes.

Brotherton Farm

As Major General Benjamin Cheatham's attack stalled and began to fold, Major General Alexander P. Stewart arrived with his Confederate division to the south of Brock field. Stewart launched an attack in support of Cheatham's left flank, where Wright's brigade had been battered in a Union counterattack. Stewart was aggressive, employing sustained offensive pressure by successively replacing his three infantry brigades into the front lines, and his troops at last broke through to the west in an assault that would scatter units of three Union divisions back across the LaFayette Road. Pursuing closely, Brigadier General Henry Clayton's brigade, supported by part of Brigadier General William Bate's on the right and Colonel John Fulton's brigade of Brigadier General Bushrod Johnson's division on the left, routed two brigades of Van Cleve's Union infantry division, along with Brigadier General William Hazen's recently withdrawn brigade and other units. This temporary breakthrough was only contained in Dyer field, several hundred yards to the west. With the survivors of a detached part of Bate's brigade reeling from a murderous artillery fire in Poe field, Clayton's and Bate's brigades of Stewart's division "fell back leisurely"[1] to the protective cover of the dense woods east of the LaFayette Road.[2]

DIRECTIONS: The Brotherton farm is designated as Tour Stop 4 on the park's auto tour route from the Visitor Center, following the route of the LaFayette Road south. For an interim visit to the scene of action on the first day of battle, continue west from Brock field on the Brotherton Road approximately 0.6 mile to the intersection of the Lafayette Road. Park on the right before reaching the intersection, facing the Brotherton house located just across the LaFayette Road.

South Ridge of Brotherton Farm

The elevated grounds of the Brotherton farm, fronting the LaFayette Road, appeared highly defensible to the hurriedly assembled Union troops and artillery forced back or drawn by the advance of Stewart's Confederate infantry in the late afternoon of September 19. In reality, as Stewart's infantry approached from the opposing smoke-filled forest on the east side of the road, with timely support on the left from Fulton's brigade, the intermingling of other Union units falling back doomed whatever chance the infantry and line of cannon on the ridge might have had.[3] Most of the monuments and markers along the crest of the ridge at the Brotherton farm trace the improvised Union line of battle that collapsed in the onrush of Stewart's attack on the first day of battle.

Poe Field

As Major General Alexander P. Stewart's division broke through near the Brotherton farm, three regiments of Bate's brigade on the right veered in pursuit of routed Union units into the southeast corner of the cornfield at the Poe farm. At the upper northeast end of the open field, and extending at an angle southwest along the tree line behind the Poe house, Major General Joseph Reynolds and Brigadier General William Hazen hurriedly assembled twenty cannon to sweep Poe field. Hazen's brigade had been withdrawn from Brock field to the vicinity of the Poe farm to replenish ammunition when Stewart's attacks began, and most of Hazen's infantry had been driven back to the west after moving to the support of Union units at the Brotherton farm. Reynolds's and Hazen's line of artillery represented a last-ditch effort to contain the spreading Confederate threat in their sector. The results proved tragic for Bate's men as canister and case-shot tore through their ranks. Within a time span of less than four minutes, with losses approaching thirty percent, Bate led the retreat back to the shelter of the forest east of the Brotherton farm.[1]

DIRECTIONS: Poe field is Stop 3 on the park's auto tour route from the Visitor Center. For an interim visit from the Brotherton farm site, turn north onto the LaFayette Road and drive 0.4 mile to the marked left turn onto Poe Road. Park at the closest pull-off just after turning onto Poe Road, and face east, or, as an alternative, walk very cautiously across the Lafayette Road to the nearby line of four south-facing cannon in the upper Poe field.

Position of Battery H, Fourth U.S. Artillery, in North Poe Field

Lieutenant Ambrose Bierce of Hazen's brigade, an eyewitness at the scene of carnage in Poe field, later wrote, "When all was over, and the dust cloud had lifted, the spectacle was too dreadful to describe."[2] The cannon in the foreground of this photograph (ca. 1896) stand where Hazen positioned Battery H, Fourth U.S. Artillery, in north Poe field, part of the hastily assembled concentration of some twenty guns as Bate's attack neared. Two cannon flank the Indiana Nineteenth Battery monument near the LaFayette Road, while the first large monument across the road and to the left, along Poe Road, represents Battery M, Fourth U.S., outlining the continuation of the line of guns. Bate later reported his loss as "at least 25 per cent . . . killed and wounded," including the wounding of all three commanding officers of the regiments and battalion engaged.[3]

West Brock Field

At an early hour, Union Colonel John T. Wilder's brigade quietly withdrew from a position east of the Viniard farm to a more defensible position across the LaFayette Road, at the wooded west border.[1] As the battle opened and spread in the north, near Jay's Mill, Bragg drew reinforcements from the accumulating large force gathering in the vicinity of Wilder's previous line. John Bell Hood's command of three Virginia brigades, supplemented by Brigadier General Bushrod Johnson's and Major General William Preston's divisions, remained idle, concealed in exceptionally dense woods east of the LaFayette Road.[2] In the early afternoon, an advance of Union Brigadier General Jefferson Davis's division struck Bushrod Johnson's front line. This ignited a long firestorm of gradually increasing combat that consumed, with heavy losses, the forces of three Confederate and three Union infantry divisions. Bushrod Johnson's division became fragmented in the smoke-filled woods as Colonel Hans Heg's brigade of Davis's division was pushed back. Fulton's brigade veered north to the vicinity of the Brotherton farm, while two other regiments advanced alone, in pursuit of routed Union units, into the open field of the west Brock farm. Approaching within eight hundred yards of Rosecrans's headquarters at the Widow Glenn's farm, these two Confederate regiments were forced into a hasty retreat by a withering enfilade fire from Wilder's position in the west Viniard field and the incoming advance of Thomas Wood's infantry division.[3]

DIRECTIONS: The open grounds of the west Brock field lie immediately north of the Viniard farm. From Tour Stop 3 at the Poe farm, follow the park's auto tour route south along the LaFayette Road approximately 0.6 mile and park on the right shoulder at the large open field near the park sign for Brigadier General Arthur M. Manigault's brigade.

View across West Brock Field

The small inscribed block of stone to the right center of this photograph is a monument to the Thirty-ninth North Carolina and Twenty-fifth Arkansas regiments of Bushrod Johnson's division, at the site of their closest approach to the Widow Glenn's farm on the afternoon of September 19. The monument stands in the west Brock field near the former site of the family cabin, several hundred yards south of the Brotherton farm and adjacent, on the north border, to the west Viniard field. The upper level of Wilder Tower, rising above the site of the Widow Glenn's cabin, can be seen above the tree line to the left.

Viniard Farm

When Brigadier General Jefferson Davis reported to General William S. Rosecrans's headquarters at the Widow Glenn's, the Union army commander hurriedly dispatched Davis's two brigades in the general direction of fighting still raging near [John] Brock field.[1] Approaching through the west Brock field in a fateful misdirection,[2] Davis's lead brigade, under the command of Colonel Hans Heg, crossed into the dense woods directly east and struck Brigadier General Bushrod Johnson's line of battle. Brigadier General William Carlin's brigade followed into the open east Viniard field, moving forward on Heg's right. Colonel John T. Wilder's brigade stood in reserve behind log and rail breastworks at the west border of the Viniard farm. In a savage, close-range firefight in woods so dense with "jack-oak bushes" that visibility was less than twenty yards,[3] Heg struggled against the slowly assembling forces of Bushrod Johnson's division. Within approximately thirty minutes, Heg ordered a fighting withdrawal, while part of Carlin's brigade hurried up in support. In Bushrod Johnson's old brigade, Brigadier General John Gregg fell wounded, superseded in command by Colonel Cyrus Sugg.

The localized fighting in dense woods spread to the open Viniard field as Major General John Bell Hood's brigades moved up in support.[4] General Braxton Bragg had earlier ordered Hood's provisional command, including the three brigades of Longstreet's corps then on hand and Johnson's division, to advance in a move designed to deflect Union attention from Major General Benjamin Cheatham's front at [John] Brock field. Through four hours of sustained and severe fighting in the vicinity of the Viniard farm, significant parts of four Union infantry divisions, with the added support of Wilder's brigade, were drawn into battle. The fighting developed in charges and countercharges through the open Viniard fields and the dense woods to the north. Union support units came up throughout the long afternoon from the vicinity of Lee and Gordon's Mill, some

two miles south. Thomas Wood's division, Colonel Sydney Barnes's brigade of Van Cleve's division, and, lastly, Sheridan's division arrived in turn at critical times when the Union lines teetered on the verge of collapse.

Bragg ordered reinforcements in support of Hood, and Colonel Robert Trigg's brigade of Major General William Preston's division moved up on the left of Brigadier General Jerome Robertson's famed Texas brigade of Hood's command. With strong support from Trigg's brigade, Robertson forced the first major collapse of the Union forces in front. Union soldiers streamed across the LaFayette Road to the protection of Wilder's fortified line at the border of the west Viniard field. Many of the Union soldiers were shot down by Confederate gunfire while taking shelter in front of Wilder's position in a shallow ravine behind the Viniard house. Robertson's advance was stopped at the long north-south line of this ditch, forcing his hasty withdrawal under the intense fire of Wilder's infantry and artillery.

When Union units counter-advanced back into the east Viniard field in the late afternoon, Hood committed his last reserve, the Georgia brigade of Brigadier General Henry "Rock" Benning. Although Benning's wide frontal attack forced an even more disorganized retreat of the Union forces to the woods behind Wilder's line, Benning's soldiers also became trapped, without support, in the ditch. Many were slaughtered by the enfilade fire of Captain Eli Lilly's artillery while pinned down by the frontal fire of Wilder's repeating rifles. As Benning withdrew his battered brigade, Union units again returned to the upper east field.

In fading daylight, Colonel Luther Bradley's brigade of Sheridan's recently arrived division attacked and was in turn driven back. Bradley suffered gunshot wounds and was replaced in command by Colonel Nathan Walworth. By late afternoon, when Sheridan's next brigade in line, Colonel Bernard Laiboldt's, arrived, the battle at the Viniard farm had ended in stalemate as both sides lay near the original lines. Heavy losses were suffered on both sides, reducing the combat effectiveness the following day of Davis's two brigades, who would be called on to fill the gap at the Brotherton farm. In Davis's lead brigade, Colonel Hans Heg was mortally wounded while regrouping his troops near the line of the infamous ditch, just north of the Viniard house, and Colonel John Martin took over command.[5]

DIRECTIONS: The Viniard farm is Tour Stop 5 on the park's auto tour route. From west Brock field, proceed south approximately 0.3 mile to the pull-off on the right.

Aerial View of Viniard Farm

Most of the grounds of the Viniard farm are visible in this aerial view (ca. 1986) from the east, the general direction of Hood's assaults. The cleared field east of Lafayette Road was more extensive in 1863.[6] Monuments cross the upper level of the east field, in front of the LaFayette Road, at some of the positions Union troops occupied at various times in a very fluid battle of east-west movements on September 19. The Viniard house was located in the very small clearing just west of the road, behind the center portion of the line of monuments. A dense growth of trees in this view, since partly cleared, conceals the north-south line of the gully behind the site of the Viniard house. Wilder's main line of battle lay along the tree line at the border of the west Viniard field, in the far background of this view. Wood's and Sheridan's divisions approached from Lee and Gordon's Mill, approximately two miles to the southeast. More heavy fighting raged in the dense woods immediately north of the east field.

East Viniard Field

Colonel John A. Martin, who succeeded Heg in brigade command following the wounding of the latter, wrote, "The stream of wounded to the rear was almost unparalleled," in his after-action report in reference to the brutality of the conflict in the dense woods east of the LaFayette Road.[7] Union monuments in this southward view across the upper grounds of the east Viniard field emphasize the prime importance of this high ground in the struggle for control of the LaFayette Road on September 19. To the right, across the road, the small glint of a park fingerpost points to the nearby site of the Viniard house. While Heg's brigade of Davis's division opened the fight, striking part of Bushrod Johnson's division in dense thickets just to the north, Carlin's brigade advanced deep into this east field. Hood attacked from the northeast, with part of Trigg's brigade later advancing from the southeast to flank the Union forces initially reinforced by Colonel George P. Buell's brigade of Wood's division. The lines of the engaged forces moved back and forth through the woods and the open fields throughout the afternoon fighting.

Eighty-first Indiana Monument and Viniard House

This photograph provides a distant glimpse of the Viniard house as it appeared in 1899, from the perspective of the Eighty-first Indiana regimental monument at the south end of monuments in the east field. This regiment of Carlin's brigade retired to Wilder's line in the west field when outflanked during Robertson's assault, then regained their initial position and held it throughout the remainder of the day, even as Benning's assault swept across the LaFayette Road. In Benning's report of the fighting, he described the Viniard farmstead as "a small house, and a smaller out-house . . . with little cover furnished by the houses, some stumps, and a few scattered trees."[8] The high rail fence behind the house became a deadly obstacle for a number of Union soldiers on the run, and the nearby ditch proved to be a death-trap for some Union and very many Confederate soldiers in the fluid battle of charge and counter-charge. A monument to the Illinois Battery C, First Light Artillery, stands on the west side of the LaFayette Road, in the left background of this view, marking a position of the unit of Sheridan's command in Bradley's late afternoon charge.

"Lost Corner School" at Viniard Farm

A log schoolhouse that stood at the western edge of wooded terrain just north of the east Viniard field became a makeshift fort for a brief time in the chaos of fighting on September 19. Heg's Union infantry brigade, advancing in an easterly direction across the LaFayette Road, passed the structure in line of battle before striking a forward line of Bushrod Johnson's division. At one point in the back-and-forth flow of battle, at the time Hood's reinforcements began to move up, a group of Fifteenth Wisconsin soldiers "gathered together in and behind a dilapidated log house built for a blacksmith's shop" in an attempt to slow the approaching infantry of Robertson's Texas brigade. The Union gunfire proved damaging for "quite a while" from the cover of a structure not readily visible to the Confederates because of the intervening trees and undergrowth, until the site was overrun.[9] This class photograph (ca. 1900) posed in front of the "Lost Corner School"[10] near the Viniard farm reveals the spacing between logs that would have enabled the Union soldiers to fire through bayonet-gouged gaps in the mud chinking.

Eli Lilly at the Site of His Battery in West Viniard Field

In this photograph of the Viniard farm (1895), which looks from the northwest, Eli Lilly, a captain of artillery in Wilder's brigade at the time of the battle, stands in the west field where a section of his battery fired enfilade rounds of double-shot canister into the ranks of Confed-

erate soldiers huddled in the shallow ditch in his front. After the battle, Wilder would say, "It actually seemed a pity to kill men so."[11] Trees and bushes were cleared extensively at the time of the park's opening, revealing a panoramic scene from the perspective of a forward position of Wilder's line of battle along the west border of the

field in front. Heg's shell monument, some 175 yards distant at right center, stands within a few feet of the generally north-south line of the gully. What appear to be the Viniard house and barn are visible beyond the shell monument. Several times in the afternoon battle, Confederate units advancing from the east Viniard field fell back below the

crest of the upper ridge for protection from Union artillery batteries along Wilder's line. The high ground of that upper ridge can be seen in the distant line of monuments placed in the east field, in the center background of this view. Lilly's wife and daughter-in-law, Mrs. J. K. Lilly, Sr. are shown sitting in the right-center foreground.[12]

Site of Lilly's Battery in West Viniard Field

Trees now obscure the distant view of monuments in the east Viniard field from the site of Lilly's Eighteenth Indiana battery in the west Viniard field. The Viniard house and outbuildings have long since been removed, and the Heg shell monument is hidden in the foliage at the right of this photograph.

John Ingraham Grave—Interlude of Battle

An overnight interlude in combat brought its own miseries as the "night was very cold and the men who were without . . . blankets suffered extremely . . . with the groans and cries of the wounded for help ringing in our sympathetic ears."[1] Heavy casualties had been suffered by both sides in the first day of battle, although accurate totals are not available. Uncounted numbers of wounded suffered untended in the woods and fields, while many of the dead had earlier been "piled upon each other in ricks, like cord wood, to make passage for advancing columns."[2] A dense fog arose in the creek bottomlands and mixed with the overhanging clouds of gun smoke. With the armies so close in the darkness, no fires were allowed, and the soldiers on each side, both wounded and able, suffered in the cold with little water near at hand.[3]

While Lieutenant General James Longstreet was en route to the battlefield, enduring a harrowing, unescorted horseback ride from the Catoosa rail station through unfamiliar territory, General Braxton Bragg reorganized the Army of Tennessee, consolidating three corps into two grand wings. From headquarters at Thedford Ford, Bragg announced to his generals that Longstreet would command the left wing, consisting of five brigades of his own Virginia command, and four additional infantry divisions. Bragg reluctantly assigned command of the right wing to his senior, though troublesome, corps commander, Lieutenant General Leonidas Polk, with four divisions and Brigadier General Nathan Bedford Forrest's cavalry.

Bragg ordered Polk to reopen the battle at sunrise, with Major General John C. Breckinridge's division leading the attack on the Union left flank, presumed to lie near Reed's Bridge Road. Polk would then follow with coordinated attacks proceeding sequentially by divisions to the left. Longstreet's command would advance as the fighting neared. The plan, developed in consideration of the piecemeal, uncoordinated nature of attack in the first day's battle, hinged on synchronized execution to roll up the Union army and drive it south, away from the approaches to Chattanooga, to destruction or to dispersal.[4] Ominously, the sound of Union axes cutting down trees for breastworks echoed through the night,[5] and a courier from Polk to Lieutenant General D. H. Hill, commanding Breckinridge's and Major General Patrick Cleburne's divisions, failed to deliver his orders for the opening attack.[6]

Rosecrans convened his late-night council of war at the small hilltop cabin of the Widow Glenn. With only two relatively fresh infantry brigades, far fewer than the number then moving up to join the Confederate ranks, and the army shaken by unusually heavy combat, the Union generals concurred that offensive action was out of the question. The army would stand in contracted lines along the LaFayette Road, the right flank completely withdrawing from the earlier scene of intense heavy fighting at the Viniard farm. New positions were drawn near the Dry Valley road, a vital route for the contingency of retreat, north to McFarland's Gap through Missionary Ridge to Chattanooga. Major General George Thomas would anchor the crucial left flank from positions then located at the Kelly farm, with his own Fourteenth Corps and other units on hand.[7]

DIRECTIONS: From the Viniard farm, turn back and retrace the incoming route, proceeding north, and turn right onto the Brotherton Road. Continue to the intersection with Alexander's Bridge Road, turn left, and proceed approximately 0.3 mile to the marked site of a trail leading to the grave of Confederate soldier John Ingraham.

John Ingraham's Grave

An inscribed tombstone surrounded by a small metal fence marks the battlefield grave site of a soldier who served in Jackson's brigade of Major General Benjamin Cheatham's division. Private John Ingraham of Company K, First Confederate Regiment, Georgia Volunteers, was killed in action near this location during the early afternoon fighting of September 19. In the aftermath of battle, his friends in the local Reed family identified the body and buried him in a marked grave where he had fallen.[8] Most of the bodies of dead soldiers of both armies were later removed to family or commemorative cemeteries, and the grave of John Ingraham remains the only positively identified burial site on the battlefield. The left fork of the trail a few steps behind the grave site leads to monuments and markers along the ridge occupied, defended, and then lost by Jackson's and Maney's brigades.

"Collecting the Wounded"

Private Sam Watkins of Company "Aytch," Maney's brigade, described the aftermath of battle: "We rested on our arms where the battle ceased. All around us everywhere were the dead and wounded, lying scattered over the ground, and in many places piled in heaps. . . . [A] detail of us were passing over the field of death and blood, with a dim lantern, looking for our wounded soldiers to carry to the hospital."[9]

William Waud, the talented but lesser known brother of Alfred, drew this scene depicting the aftermath of an engagement near Hatcher's Run, Virginia, during the siege of Petersburg, October 1864, but its portrayal of the grim human toll of battle also relates to the dark woodland activity after the battle of Chickamauga.

McDonald Farm—Approaches to Kelly Field

Confederate Lieutenant General Leonidas Polk awoke in the foggy predawn darkness of September 20 to find that his orders to Lieutenant General D. H. Hill for a sunrise attack had not been delivered. Although Major General John C. Breckinridge's division of Hill's corps had moved up to an assigned battle station in the woods just south of Reed's Bridge Road, the other units of Polk's new wing command were considerably out of position and unprepared. Four hours of daylight were lost before the troops were assembled near the front. As Bragg grew increasingly anxious over the lost opportunity, the Union soldiers of George Thomas's command used the respite to strengthen and complete their line of opposing breastworks at the Kelly farm.[1]

Thomas had chosen the ground along the crest of a broad ridge in the woods just east of Kelly field to establish his fortified main position for the expected renewal of battle. Despite repeated requests that Brigadier General James Negley's detached infantry division move up from the south and fill the gap of several hundred yards north to the McDonald farm crossroads, only one brigade arrived in time. As the first Confederate attack force neared, Thomas deployed Brigadier General John Beatty's brigade to the left of Baird's terminating line of breastworks near the LaFayette Road, overextending Beatty's troops.[2]

When the battle reopened at 9:30 A.M., two Indiana regiments and three cannon of Captain Lyman Bridge's Illinois battery stood isolated on the high ground of the McDonald house as Breckinridge's Confederate division approached on a broad front through the woods from the east, in line of battle extending south from Reed's Bridge Road. Beatty's thin line of defense collapsed in the onrush of Breckinridge's infantry, with part of Brigadier General Benjamin Helm's brigade breaking through the lines of Beatty's other regiments near the intersection of Alexander's Bridge Road.[3]

Despite the earlier extended delay, the opening drive of the Confederate offensive with Breckinridge's division temporarily succeeded in breaching the Union left flank. Major General Daniel W. Adams and Brigadier General Marcellus Stovall turned their brigades south in the McDonald fields, advancing in line of battle abreast of the LaFayette Road to Kelly field, and gained the rear of Thomas's line of breastworks east of the Kelly house.

Negley's Union brigades fought hard, delaying the advance of Stovall and Adams just long enough to allow Van Derveer's brigade and other units to come up from reserve positions. Adams was wounded and captured at the front of his troops in thick woods west of the Kelly field. Without support at the front, Breckinridge's flank attack collapsed under heavy fire, leading to a withdrawal to the original point of departure east of the LaFayette Road.

Hill dispatched Govan's brigade of St. John Liddell's division in a belated attempt to reinforce Breckinridge's attack. Govan's brigade followed in Breckinridge's path and also reached the open Kelly field behind Thomas's lines before withdrawing in the face of enveloping counterattacks. This second unsupported Confederate attack along the LaFayette Road succeeded in dispersing two Union infantry brigades in the approach. One of these fragmented units, under the command of Colonel Timothy R. Stanley of Negley's division, retreated to the west, in the direction of the Snodgrass farm, for a later role in the battle.[4]

DIRECTIONS: The approach route of Breckinridge's division in the opening of the second day of battle can be viewed from the high ground of the Visitor Center or from Tour Stop 1 on the park's auto tour route. From the site of John Ingraham's grave, continue northwest along Alexander's Bridge Road to the intersection with the LaFayette Road. Turn right, and proceed north a short distance to the parking area on the left at the park's Tour Stop 1.

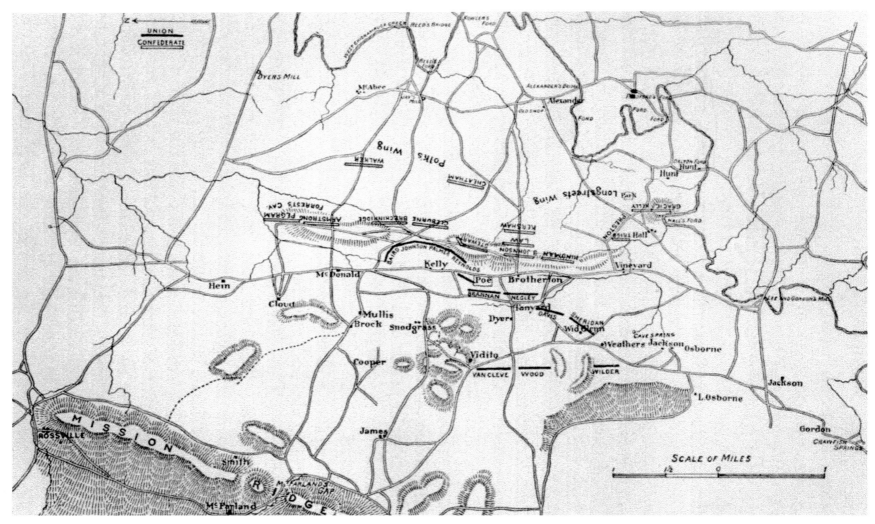

Opening Dispositions at the Battle of Chickamauga, September 20, 1863

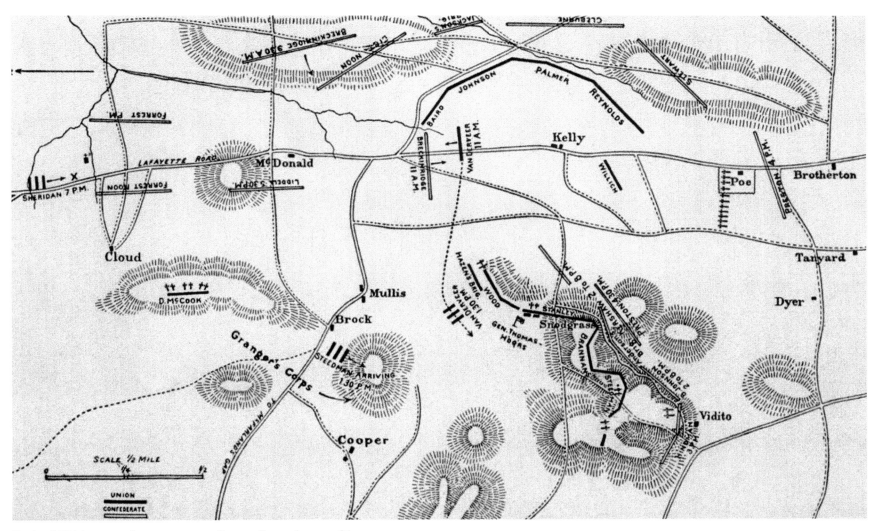

Battle of Chickamauga from 9:30 A.M. to Sunset, September 20, 1863

Breckinridge's Approach Route to Kelly Field

This modern photograph was taken from the lower grounds of the Visitor Center, below the former site of the McDonald house, and shows a view to the south. To the left, across the LaFayette Road, the cupola of the Florida monument stands in the staging area where two Florida infantry regiments, part of Stovall's brigade, wheeled to the left and began the advance south along the left of the road. Adam's brigade, after dispersing the Union troops of Beatty's brigade at the site of the McDonald house, also wheeled to the left to begin their advance on the right of the road.

In the middle right distance, by the large tree, four cannon represent the forward position of Captain C.H. Slocomb's Louisiana battery on the next rise of ground. On the left of the road, some two hundred yards farther south, the tall column of the Kentucky monument stands nearly opposite the site where four cannon (unseen in this view) represent an earlier position of another section of Bridge's Illinois battery, at a site near where Kentucky soldiers of both sides struggled in combat. Just beyond is a glimpse of the northwest corner of Kelly field, where Stovall's brigade reached the open ground behind the Union breastworks.

Slocomb's Battery and Florida Monument

Four cannon representing the position of Slocomb's Louisiana battery (the famed Washington artillery) stand on a rise of ground just south of the Visitor Center, with the state of Florida's monument across the road. When Breckinridge attacked on September 20, the battery stood in front of an orchard on the lower grounds of the McDonald farm, providing covering fire for the advance and later retreat of Adam's and Stovall's brigades. In the retreat of Adam's brigade, Slocomb reported "fine" results from waiting until the infantry had "gained the ravine in my immediate front before opening fire on pursuing Federal units."[5] Florida's monument, with its distinctive cupola, stands near where two Florida regiments, part of Stovall's brigade, participated in the advance toward Kelly field. The site of the battery is designated as the park's first tour stop on the auto driving tour route.

Site of Confederate Breakthrough in Northwest Kelly Field

This photograph (ca. 1895) provides a view of the ground in the northwest corner of Kelly field where Stovall's brigade of Breckinridge's division broke into the rear of the Union lines. Telegraph poles line the LaFayette Road, to the left, along the border of the relatively open west woods where Adam's brigade actually reached even farther south. At the time of Breckinridge's incursion into Kelly field, heavy fighting had broken out along the left of Baird's fortified Union lines to the east, in the woods to the right. Artillery on the slight rise of ground in front and reinforcements from the left and right turned the tide for the embattled northern flank of the Union army. Van Derveer's brigade emerged from the woods to the west, crossing the road and pivoting north, in front of the posted gun batteries, to confront Breckinridge's emerging line.[6]

Kelly Farm and Vicinity

Parts of Major General John C. Breckinridge's left brigade, led by Brigadier General Benjamin Helm, opened the battle on September 20 by striking the Union line of log breastworks from the east at one of the strongest points, the northernmost angle where Baird's division manned a section of works turned back in a westerly direction. Much of Helm's brigade was shattered with heavy losses in a series of frontal assaults across open ground against fieldworks concealing Union soldiers firing through gaps in the logs. Helm was shot down with a mortal wound in front of the Union lines while leading a third assault. Colonel Peyton H. Colquitt, leading a fresh brigade of Brigadier General States Rights Gist's division in delayed support of Helm's attack, was also killed in action, 365 feet to the west of the site where Helm had fallen.[1]

At 10 A.M., Lieutenant General D. H. Hill ordered Major General Patrick Cleburne's division forward in support on the left of Helm's frontal attacks. Cleburne's crack division struggled to maintain formations over rough terrain through dense forest against breastworks manned by Palmer's and Reynolds's Union infantry divisions. Cleburne later reported: "I was now within short canister range of a line of log breastworks, and a hurricane of shot and shell swept the woods from the unseen enemy in my front."[2] On Cleburne's right, the brigade of Lucius Polk, nephew to Wing Commander Leonidas Polk, was stopped by concentrated frontal and enfilade fire at a distance of 175 yards in front of the Union line. On Cleburne's left, Wood's brigade attacked to the line of the LaFayette Road across the open ground of Poe field, passing, under heavy frontal and flank fire, the southern end of the Kelly field line manned by Reyn-

olds's division, where it bent back west. Wood's attack failed, as did Brigadier General James Deshler's later frontal assault on the line of breastworks to the left of Lucius Polk's brigade. Deshler was killed at the front at the time Cleburne ordered all units to take cover in the shelter of a ridge several hundred yards from the Union breastworks.[3]

Leonidas Polk continued the fight through the hour of noon with an inexplicably piecemeal and uncoordinated deployment of the remaining units of Major General William H. T. Walker's reserve corps. During this time, Major General Benjamin Cheatham's large division, under Leonidas Polk's wing command, remained uncommitted near the scene of the previous day's battle at Brock field. Although Confederate striking power had shaken Major General George Thomas's position, particularly near the LaFayette Road, and brought much of the Union right streaming to the left in support, General Braxton Bragg was distraught at the pattern of Polk's troop deployment, with heavy losses and no visible advantage gained. The opportunity to seize the LaFayette Road and drive the Union army south seemed to be disappearing. By 11:00 A.M., with his frustration piqued, Bragg dispatched couriers to every division commander in the field with direct orders to advance without delay.[4]

DIRECTIONS: From the park's Tour Stop 1 at the site of Slocomb's battery, return south to the intersection of Alexander's Bridge Road, marked by the tall Kentucky monument on the southeast corner, turn left, and follow the road markings to the sign indicating a right turn onto Battle Line Road at Tour Stop 2.

Aerial View of Kelly and Snodgrass Fields

A few hundred yards of wooded terrain separate Kelly field from the open field of Snodgrass farm in this westward view of the battlefield from the perspective of the Kelly farm. A log cabin surrounded by a picket fence marks the site of the Kelly house, at the left border of the lower open field. To the right, monuments mark the positions of Union and Confederate forces in the crisis of Breckinridge's attack. The outline of Battle Line Road can be detected in the heavy woods just below the Kelly field.

Battle Line Road is a tour roadway created by the park to follow the line of Union forces along the outer perimeter of the Kelly farm. During the climactic struggle on Snodgrass Hill, while four Union divisions remained in position behind the barricades at the Kelly farm, Longstreet approached from the southwest under fire to reconnoiter the wooded corridor between the two Union positions. Longstreet ordered Buckner to prepare a line of twelve cannon at the Poe farm to enfilade Union lines at the Kelly farm and control access to the critical LaFayette Road.[5]

Baird's Angle at Battle Line Road

Baird's fortified position at the northern end of Thomas's Kelly farm line of battle turned sharply back to the west. Monuments and markers along Battle Line Road trace the outline where Union units fought, firing from the protection of log barricades fortified with rocks and broken tree limbs. The left of Helm's brigade, a few hundred strong, first struck this section of the works and was shattered in successive attacks. Helm was mortally wounded in the third assault, in open woods near the clearing in front of the Union works at a distance of some 800 feet. Throughout the morning assaults, Confederate infantry pressed forward no closer than forty yards to the fortified Union lines.[6]

Log and Rail Barricades on Union Left

This sculpted detail on the First Battalion, Nineteenth U.S. Infantry monument at Baird's angle of the Kelly farm perimeter line depicts a prone soldier firing through a gap in stacked logs. Fence rails and broken tree limbs were jammed between the stacked logs, at right angles, to provide a gap for musket fire. In many sections of the barricades, as this detail on the monument shows, the logs were laid crosswise for added protection against enfilade fire. Brigadier General John King, whose brigade of U.S. regular infantry manned this sector, reported the log breastworks as two feet in height.[7]

Baird's Angle from Site of Colquitt Shell Monument

Confederate Colonel Peyton Colquitt, in temporary command of a brigade in Gist's reserve division, was mortally wounded at this site, just below the crest of the sloping ground on the north end of the Kelly farm perimeter line, while following in the path of Helm's earlier advance. This photograph, viewing west from the vicinity where Colquitt was shot, provides a view of the slope up to the clearing in front of Baird's position at the northern angle in the Union lines along the wooded east perimeter of the Kelly farm. The upper part of one of the monuments at the distant site of Baird's position, representing the fighting line of the Tenth Wisconsin regiment, can be seen to the left of the two trees partially blocking the park marker tablet. The visible part of the Wisconsin monument bears the figure of a soldier holding a flag. The forward momentum of both Colquitt's and, earlier, Helm's charging units ended near the upper ground in front, in a clearing in front of the Union lines. The park tablet, at left center, marks a position of Helm's earlier assault, while the small stone monument to the right represents a forward position of the Twenty-fourth South Carolina Regiment of Colquitt's brigade. The shell monument where Colquitt fell lies out of view, just a few steps east from the spot where this photograph, looking west, was taken, while a similar monument where Helm fell lies 365 feet farther east along the park trail.

Site of Battle Line Road—Early Park View

A transitional phase of park development is evident in this photograph (ca. 1895) of monuments along the crest of the low ridge east of Kelly field, prior to the grading of what would become Battle Line Road, on the line of General Thomas's fortified position at the Kelly farm on the second day of battle. These monuments mark positions of Union infantry and artillery near the junction of barricades manned by Baird's and Richard Johnson's divisions. The guns of the Fifth Indiana Battery, represented by the monument and cannon in the center of this view, fired more than twelve hundred rounds in the daylong battle with the Confederates of Polk's wing, particularly Cleburne's division.[8]

Hazen's Position at Kelly Farm from Confederate Perspective

Two cannon and a monument at a front line position of Brigadier General William Hazen's brigade, Richard Johnson's division, are just visible in the background of this view from the east, below the high ground of the Union lines. Here Confederate infantry of Cleburne's division assaulted Union lines, contending with a strong infantry force posted behind a line of log breastworks that enabled enfilade fire, ably supported with artillery firing short-range canister. Cleburne's frontal attacks collapsed at forward positions no closer than 175 yards from the breastworks on the morning of September 20.[9] The trail in the foreground of this view leads east, in the opposite direction, to a series of opposing, lower ridges, where the men of Deshler's brigade took shelter on the back slopes after suffering exposure to the deadly fire. On the crest of the first lower ridge east, a shell monument marks the site where Deshler was killed instantly by a cannonball striking through his chest, the third Confederate general officer to be killed that day. Hazen reported a loss of only thirteen men in the attacks on his section of breastworks, while the corresponding Confederate losses totaled in the hundreds.[10]

Hazen's Position along Modern Battle Line Road

In this modern, northeastward view of a segment of Hazen's position, the monument in the foreground, flanked by two twelve-pounder Napoleons, marks the position of Battery F, First Ohio Light Artillery. On the previous day of battle, this battery saw heavy action at Brock field and, later, at the Poe farm. At this position three hundred feet east of Kelly field, the battery fired a total of 185 rounds in the repulse of three distinct Confederate assaults.[11]

Colonel Edward King Monument at Kelly Field

Colonel Edward A. King, whose brigade anchored Reynolds's adjusted right flank in the woods at the south end of Kelly field, was killed by a sharpshooter late in the afternoon of September 20. A shell monument marks the spot where he fell, approximately eight hundred feet east of the now reconstructed Kelly cabin.

Wounded Union soldiers were tended in and around the Kelly house on the outer perimeter of battle until the structures were set afire in the late afternoon fighting. Monuments and markers to the right of this view denote positions of Confederate and hastily deployed Union artillery and infantry units at the time of Breckinridge's morning incursion into the north Kelly field.[12]

Poe Farm

In the early morning hours of September 20, Brigadier General Brannan deployed the brigades of Croxton and Connell in the cover of log and rail breastworks masked by heavy timber and undergrowth.[1] Brannan's position stretched around behind the Poe house, at the center junction of Union lines crossing over the LaFayette Road to the west side. To the north, Reynolds's division manned the south line of the Kelly farm position, while Thomas Wood's division joined on the right at the Brotherton farm. Van Derveer's brigade had been posted in reserve in Dyer field to the west.[2]

When Thomas, at the critical moment of Major Breckinridge's approach to Kelly field, requested support from Brannan's division, the field commanders at the critical junction hesitated to create a gap.[3] Brannan dispatched Van Derveer's brigade from its reserve position, and Reynolds's moved Colonel Edward King's brigade across the LaFayette Road to strengthen Brannan's left. A courier rode to Rosecrans's new headquarters in south Dyer field behind the Brotherton farm and reported his perception of the changing dispositions. In the confusion, while shifting multiple army units from the right to the then threatened left, Rosecrans was led to believe Brannan's entire division had moved north, creating a serious gap at the hinge of the Union lines.[4] At the hour of 10:45 A.M., just prior to Alexander P. Stewart's Confederate attack, orders were hastily drafted and dispatched to Wood, at the Brotherton farm line, that would prove catastrophic to the fate of the Union army at Chickamauga: "The general commanding directs that you close up on Reynolds as fast as possible, and support him."[5]

Just before 11:00 A.M., as the battle on Leonidas Polk's front neared the right of Longstreet's wing, General Braxton Bragg's preemptory orders for advance reached Stewart, whose division was located east of the Poe farm. Longstreet was caught off guard by the premature launching of the right flank of his left wing command and hurried final preparations to commit his adjoining column of assault.[6] There would be no time for Longstreet to support Stewart. His three brigades moved without delay, coming under fire from the start of their advance, launched from a low ridge in open woods opposite Brannan's line of breastworks behind the Poe house.

On Stewart's right, as the attack formed to cross the open Poe field, part of Brigadier General S. A. M. Wood's brigade of Cleburne's division advanced under severe flank fire from the breastworks of Turchin's Union brigade at the southwest angle of the Kelly farm line. A Confederate officer commanding the Forty-fifth Regiment, Alabama Volunteers, later reported: "I gave the order to retreat. . . . [W]e could not see the enemy, and did not return the fire."[7] Stewart's three brigades were also exposed to heavy artillery and musket fire from the front and both flanks. Although some Confederate units entered the breastworks behind the burning Poe house, what Stewart described as the "most terrible fire it has ever been my fortune to witness"[8] forced a quick withdrawal of all units to the shelter of the ridges several hundred yards back to the east. At the time Stewart withdrew, Longstreet's main column of assault had just moved forward towards the Brotherton farm, to the south of Poe field.[9]

DIRECTIONS: The park's Tour Stop 3, Poe farm, is located on Poe Road, the extension of Battle Line Road across the LaFayette Road, approximately one mile from Tour Stop 2.

Aerial View of Poe Farm

Heavy fighting erupted in the vicinity of Larkin Poe's small farm on both days of the battle. In this aerial view, looking west, the wider open field in the lower foreground is Poe field, while the smaller plot on the east side of the LaFayette Road surrounds the former site of the Poe house. In the late afternoon of September 19, Bate's brigade of Stewart's division advanced obliquely across Poe field from the south end, emerging near the site where the tall Georgia monument would later be erected. Federal artillery posted on both sides of the LaFayette Road broke the attack with volleys of canister and case shot. On the morning of September 20, Stewart's entire division attacked across Poe field from the east, confronting Brannan's brigades in the woods to the west, behind the Poe house, and Reynolds's enfilade fire from the south end of the Kelly farm perimeter line.

North Dyer field, the scene of later fighting on September 20, lies just beyond the woods west of Poe's in the more distant background of this aerial view.

Modern View of Poe Field from Reynolds's Line

Looking south across Poe field from the position of Battery H, Fourth U.S. Artillery, the tall Georgia monument stands approximately 450 yards distant, near the area where Bate's onrushing line of battle broke into the open field on September 19. Battery H fired lethal blasts of case shot and canister, with a rated effective range of up to four hundred yards. Bate's two right regiments found themselves within killing range from the moment they crossed into the field. On the following day, when Stewart's entire division attacked from east to west across the length of the field, Battery H had been withdrawn to a position near the Kelly house, but Reynolds's and Brannan's recessed artillery and small-arms fire raked Poe field in a crossfire. Beyond the stop sign in the photo, foliage masks the line of monuments and cannon along Poe Road.

A depression in Poe field, beginning where the park tablet lies just beyond the roadway in the foreground, provided Stewart's infantry some protection from Reynolds's enfilade fire.[10]

Union and Confederate Guns at the Site of Poe House

The site of Larkin Poe's farmhouse, the "burning house" of many Confederate reports, is bordered by cannon of both armies representing positions at different times in the battle.[11] In this view, looking southeast from the position of Battery D, First Michigan Light Artillery, along Poe Road, the small park fingerpost marking the site of the Poe house stands just left of the base of the more distant Georgia monument. The dark border woodland seen behind the monument currently blocks the view through open woods that Union artillery units used to target Stewart's original position, along a low ridge several hundreds yards farther to the east, on the morning of September 20.[12] Battery D marks the position of Connell's brigade at Brannan's fortified Poe farm line that was briefly overrun in Stewart's attack. The line of north-facing cannon to the right and center of this view represent Confederate artillery assembled by Major General Buckner as it was subsequently positioned towards the Union lines at Kelly field.

Position of Battery M, Fourth U.S. Artillery, at Poe Farm

These cannon were part of the deadly array of Union field artillery facing Alexander P. Stewart's Confederate infantry at the Poe farm on both days of the battle. Union monuments at the site of the Poe farm were located, at the time of the opening of the park, in open woods with more visibility of the entire position than that encountered by modern visitors.

Brotherton Farm

Lieutenant General James Longstreet used the four hours of delayed advance of Polk's right wing to methodically prepare his left wing command for a concentrated assault. Whether by design or by coincidence of troop placement, Longstreet's wing was ideally configured to avoid the piecemeal pattern of attack that developed to his right. Three infantry divisions were stacked in a compact formation of five lines abreast of the Brotherton Road, beginning six hundred yards east of the Brotherton house, under direct field command of Major General John Bell Hood. Although Alexander P. Stewart's division on the right foundered in the premature attack through Poe field, Longstreet retained Major General Thomas C. Hindman's division to Hood's immediate left, with Preston's division in reserve south of the Viniard farm.[1]

At 11:10 A.M., Longstreet signaled the advance of his wing command at a time when the odds were heavily in his favor. Most of the remaining units of the Union right were then in motion to the northern flank. Compounding the situation, Brigadier General Thomas Wood had chosen to promptly obey Rosecrans's confusing order based on the erroneous assumption of a gap at Brannan's Poe field line.[2] Wood withdrew his division in rear of the Brotherton farm to march around Brannan to Reynolds's line at Kelly field, creating an actual half-mile gap in the Union lines.

As Wood's trailing brigade completed the evacuation, two brigades of Jefferson Davis's division began shifting left to reach the empty breastworks.[3] By then it was too late. Units of Brigadier General Bushrod Johnson's division, in the forward ranks of Hood's center formation, had already crossed the LaFayette Road in front of the Brotherton house. Despite galling fire from Union batteries and infantry on the flanks, Johnson's two lead brigades fanned out across the narrow field behind the Brotherton house, leaping over the empty log works at the tree line and dispersing the lead brigade of Davis's Union division just as it arrived.

On Johnson's right, Evander McNair's brigade stalled in the face of stiff opposition from Brannan's two brigades at Poe farm, until Colonel Cyrus A. Sugg's reserve brigade and Benning's brigade of Hood's third line came up in support. On Johnson's left, Hindman's division joined in the Confederate advance and widened the breakthrough, routing the other brigade of Davis's division. Pursuing through the quarter-mile deep stretch of woods behind the Union breastworks, the Confederates broke into Dyer field and scattered Buell's trailing brigade of Wood's division.[4]

Rosecrans witnessed the chaotic scene in front of his new headquarters as Confederate infantry broke into the Dyer field just behind the routed units of Davis's Union division, forcing a rapid ride to the south to coordinate a response.[5] The three brigades of Sheridan's division, Wilder's mounted infantry brigade, and a handful of other small units were approaching from the south to attempt a containment of the breakthrough as Buell's brigade broke up and the troops fled west.

DIRECTIONS: The park's Tour Stop 4, Brotherton farm, is located on the west side of the LaFayette Road, approximately two hundred yards south of the exit junction of Poe Road.

Modern View of Brotherton Cabin

One of the signature landmarks of Chickamauga battlefield, the reconstructed Brotherton house stands on the west side of the LaFayette Road at the intersection with the Brotherton Road, at the focal scene where the climactic Confederate breakthrough began. This view is from the southwest, behind the cabin. Union pickets posted along a rail fence in front were the first to see Longstreet's advance infantry appear in the last bend of the Brotherton Road.[6] Colonel John Fulton, commanding the center brigade in Bushrod Johnson's division, reported the scene: "[C]rossing the fence, the engagement became general. Here we passed a house and garden. . . . On entering the house, cribs, etc., many prisoners [wounded], both officers and men, were captured, and here some fine swords were taken."[7] The two rifled cannon facing west, in the foreground of this view, represent a position of Bledsoe's Missouri battery; two cannon on the other side of the cabin stand at the position of Culpepper's South Carolina battery. Neither battery advanced with Bushrod Johnson's infantry during the opening phase of Longstreet's breakthrough attack.[8]

The Brotherton Cabin

This photograph (ca. 1896) captures a perspective of the Brotherton house, attached rear structure, and barn, viewing southwest from the lower level of the LaFayette Road. On the morning of September 20, the Union line of breast-works along the north-south ridge of Brotherton field faced the LaFayette Road from the woods at the west border, which were approximately seventy-five yards behind the house at this point.

Union soldiers of Buell's brigade, in the center of Wood's defensive line of works, posted skirmishers near the fence in front of the cabin to slow any Confederate advance; the elevated shoulder of ground at the roadside and the woods to the east would have concealed any approach to the Union lines located behind the cabin. Longstreet's initial attack did approach basically unseen through the woods directly east of the Brotherton farm.

"Longstreet's Soldiers Debarking from Trains below Ringgold, September 18, 1863"

Alfred R. Waud's pen and ink rendering captures the scene on September 18, 1863, at Catoosa Station, the available north terminus of the Western and Atlantic Railroad for the Confederate army at the time of the battle. Five of the nine brigades sent from Longstreet's First Corps of the Army of Northern Virginia arrived in time to take part in the battle, trickling in at staggered intervals because of the overstrained Confederate rail system. Robertson's brigade of Hood's former division arrived first, on September 17. Waud's illustration depicts a scene on the day when two brigades of Hood's old division "debarked."

View along Brotherton Road Where Longstreet's Infantry Formed

Park tablets along the Brotherton Road some four hundred yards east of the Brotherton cabin indicate assembly positions of infantry units in Longstreet's "grand column" of assault. Under Hood's immediate command, three infantry divisions totaling some eleven thousand men were compressed into a stacked formation in thick woods, with a front some seven hundred yards in width.[9] The breadth of Hood's front only slightly exceeded the open frontage of Brotherton field. Bushrod Johnson's division occupied the lead position, with two brigades forward and one supporting. Brevet Brigadier General Gates P. Thruston, a lieutenant colonel in McCook's Union corps at the time of the battle, later wrote, "Wave after wave of Confederates came on; resistance only increased the multitude."[10]

West Brock Field

Brigadier General Arthur M. Manigault led his Confederate brigade, on the left of Hindman's division, through the virtually undefended area of the west Brock field in the advance of Lieutenant General James Longstreet's wing at approximately 11:30 A.M.[1] The hilltop site of the Widow Glenn's cabin was a key to gaining control of the nearby Dry Valley road. Manigault approached at a time when little opposition existed at the commanding elevation, which overlooked, to the west, the road from Crawfish Springs that was then serving as a principal route of retreat for Union forces. After part of Manigault's command nearly broke through at the farmyard next to the burning Glenn cabin, Wilder's brigade and other incoming units approached on the run and launched a series of frontal and flank counterattacks. Manigault was forced to lead his battered brigade back under intense pressure through the open fields of their earlier approach.[2] At the LaFayette Road, with trailing units still under fire and closely pursued, Trigg's brigade of Preston's Confederate reserve division came up to the roadside in support, and Wilder withdrew to the west. Manigault's brigade reformed for an alternative route of advance to the northwest in support of the Confederate breakthrough.[3]

DIRECTIONS: The west Brock field is the first large open field to the south of the Brotherton farm, approximately 0.5 miles south of Tour Stop 4.

View from Widow Glenn's Farm

On the second day of battle, on the left flank of Longstreet's assault, Manigault's brigade of Hindman's division advanced unchecked through the west Brock field to a major confrontation at the Widow Glenn's farm before turning back in defeat with some regiments under close pursuit by Wilder's troops. This photograph (ca. 1890) from the grounds of the Widow Glenn's cornfield at the base of the hill, looking east, provides a view of Manigault's approach from the perspective of the small force of Union troops initially on hand for defense. Wilder's dismounted infantry charged from the southeast through an open field "thickly studded with girdlings—dead trees," out of view to the right of this photograph.[4]

Widow Glenn's Farm

In the early morning hours of September 19, as the distant sounds of developing battle to the northeast signified a major engagement, General Rosecrans moved his headquarters from the Widow Gordon's house at Crawfish Springs to a more tactically central location, three miles north, at the hilltop cabin of a widowed young woman named Eliza Glenn.[1] When Union lines directly to the east first began to break in the midafternoon struggle surrounding the Viniard farm, and two Confederate regiments approached within eight hundred yards through the west Brock field, the "roar of battle" reached the Union commander's headquarters.[2] The Eighth Wisconsin Artillery Battery and the Fifteenth Pennsylvania Cavalry Escort provided the only forces immediately at hand for defense, until Wilder's flank fire from the west Viniard field stopped the Confederate advance.[3] Rosecrans convened a late-night council of war with his field commanders inside the Widow Glenn's cabin, where the decision was made to stand and fight on the following day with contracted lines of battle.[4]

Rosecrans and his staff rode north in the early morning fog of September 20 to inspect the newly established lines and choose a more centrally located headquarters site in Dyer field, less than a mile north of the Glenn farm.[5] Sheridan positioned his infantry division on ridgelines in front of and behind the Widow Glenn's farm, straddling the Dry Valley road. Wilder's mobile reserve brigade formed a new line on his right, a quarter-mile southwest of Glenn hill.

By 11:00 A.M., Sheridan's three brigades were moving north in support of the army's ongoing shift to the left.[6] Wilder's brigade and the Thirty-ninth Indiana Regiment, another unit of mounted infantry armed with Spencer repeaters, prepared to fill the gap left by Sheridan's departure. Within thirty minutes, Manigault's Confederate brigade, on the left of Hindman's division, began the advance through the west Brock field and approached the Widow Glenn's farm at a time when only fragments of Sheridan's command remained near the hilltop.

Manigault had broken through on the wooded heights to the right, with another regiment maneuvering on the left, but his frontal charge up the open slopes met an unexpected rapid-firing charge from the Thirty-ninth Indiana, coming in from the west, at the hilltop. The Widow Glenn's log cabin had just exploded into flames in the crash of a bursting artillery shell. At this time of confusion on the smoke-shrouded hill, Wilder's dismounted infantry charged into the open Glenn field behind the Confederate infantry on Manigault's left with sustained and rapid, repeating rifle volleys. Amid the overwhelming crossfire, with growing numbers of Confederate soldiers fleeing back through the fields of their earlier approach, Manigault ordered a withdrawal, under close pursuit by Wilder's troops.

Manigault's retreat reached the LaFayette Road before Trigg's brigade of Preston's division came up in support and Wilder withdrew.[7] Lieutenant General James Longstreet later admitted that he thought an entire infantry corps had struck his left flank when he heard the distant uproar of the rapid-firing Spencers.[8]

DIRECTIONS: Wilder Tower and the Widow Glenn's farm, the park's Tour Stop 6, are located on the Glenn-Viniard Road, approximately 2.8 miles from the Brotherton farm via the park's marked tour route. Just past Tour Stop 5, turn right from the LaFayette Road onto Glenn-Viniard Road and proceed to the parking area for Tour Stop 6.

Modern View of Wilder Tower

Wilder Tower stands atop the hill at the Widow Glenn's farm, flanked by monuments commemorating events of both days of battle. In the foreground of this view from the southeast, the obelisk of the Eighth Wisconsin Battery monument, with two cannon, marks the battery's position on September 19 as it defended Rosecrans's hilltop headquarters site against the approach through the west Brock field of two straying units of McNair's Confederate brigade. At the upper left of this view from the southeast, the angular-shaped Twenty-first Michigan Infantry Detachment's monument, partially hidden by the hilltop tree to the left of the tower in this view, commemorates the holding action of this unit, attached to Sheridan's command at the time, on September 20, when Manigault's brigade drew near. A smaller monument to the immediate right of the tower's base marks the position of a front line of the Thirty-ninth Indiana Mounted Infantry Regiment, which fought dismounted in the smoke and heat of the burning Glenn cabin.[9] Wilder's brigade advanced from the southwest and struck the left flank of Manigault's reeling infantry in the cultivated field at the base of the hill.

Wilder Tower at Site of Widow Glenn's Cabin

In the upper background of this photograph (ca. 1896), viewing from the west, the partially completed stone tower erected in memory of Wilder's "Lightning Brigade" rises from the former site of the Widow Glenn's cabin. Construction began in 1892, and the memorial tower rose to the sixty-foot height seen in this photograph until work was suspended for several years. Wilder Tower, as it is generally known, was completed to the full eighty-five-foot height in 1899.[10] Monuments in the lower foreground represent various Union units whose roles in the battle occurred outside of the park boundaries. From the next ridge west, in rear of this view, the Thirty-ninth Indiana Mounted Infantry Brigade rushed forward, dismounted, to confront Manigault's advance at the top of Glenn Hill.

Diorama of Rosecrans Interrogating Prisoners in the Widow Glenn's Cabin

This scene from a diorama previously located in the Lookout Mountain Museum near Point Park depicts General William S. Rosecrans interrogating captured Confederates inside the Widow Glenn's log cabin on the first day of battle. Wilder Tower stands a few steps south of the hilltop site of Eliza Glenn's cabin, "a small log structure, with porch on the north side and a large stone chimney at one end. . . . The group of small buildings, corn, cribs [sic] and stables were demolished and the material placed in the defenses [by Union soldiers of Lytle's brigade, early on September 20], the chinking between the logs of the house knocked out and a detail placed within to fire between the logs."[11] The Widow Glenn's cabin was destroyed by shell fire during the later approach of Manigault's brigade. In the late evening hours of September 19, Rosecrans convened a council of war inside the cabin. The scene was recorded by Captain W. C. Margedant, a staff topographical engineer: "Widow Glenn's log house was, like all the houses of that kind, provided with a large fire-place, in which a bright fire was burning—perhaps the only fire within 15 square miles, on account of the order given not to light fires on that night for any purpose. The remains of a candle were stuck into a reversed bayonet, lighting up dimly the battle map, which was spread out upon a cartridge box."[12]

West of Widow Glenn's Cabin

A line of monuments along the Crawfish Springs Road, at the rear base of the hill at the Widow Glenn's, commemorates various Union units whose contributions to the battle occurred outside of the later park boundaries. In this view (ca. 1895) to the northwest, the Thirty-ninth Indiana Regiment of mounted infantry, posted for rear echelon defense by Sheridan on the hillside in the background, advanced dismounted across the road and up to the Widow Glenn's cabin to confront leading elements of Manigault's command. The road leads to Bloody Pond some four hundred yards northwest.

Bloody Pond

The battle of Chickamauga occurred at a time of severe drought in the north Georgia region. Water for the parched soldiers of both armies remained scarce. Although Confederate soldiers had a ready supply available from Chickamauga Creek, which flowed behind their lines throughout the two days of battle, the long walks required from the front lines diminished availability, acutely for the wounded. Union troops wounded in battle and transported some two miles south, to the field hospitals in and around the Gordon-Lee mansion, fared somewhat better, with the nearby water of Crawfish Springs in abundant supply. Elsewhere, Union soldiers suffered for two days with no other source of water than the stagnant cattle pond located beside the Dry Valley road just north of the Widow Glenn's farm.[1] The pond banks became filled with wounded men and animals whose blood is said to have stained the water red.

Wilder's brigade, mounted on horseback, rode three hundred yards north to the pond after their withdrawal from the Widow Glenn's farm on September 20: "We here secured water for our famished thirsty men, from among dead men & mules who had fallen, wounded [,] in the mud trying to quench the awful thirst of death, from its reeking contents."[2] Confederate soldiers of Brigadier General Zachariah C. Deas's and Brigadier General Patton Anderson's brigades of Hindman's division had already passed the site of Bloody Pond, as it became known, in their pursuit of the scattered units of Sheridan's Union division through the network of foothills fronting Missionary Ridge to the west. Hindman broke off the chase of Sheridan's routed command after pursuing for three-quarters of a mile and turned north in response to orders from Lieutenant General James Longstreet to close up on the left of Brigadier General Bushrod Johnson's division.[3]

DIRECTIONS: From the site of Wilder Tower at Tour Stop 6, proceed to the nearby intersection of the Chickamauga-Vittetoe Road. Turn left and proceed approximately 0.25 mile to the monuments and parking area behind Wilder Tower. Turn right, crossing the railroad tracks, and turn right again onto Lytle Road. Continue north approximately four hundred yards, and park on the right shoulder of the road at the (presently) unmarked site of Bloody Pond, immediately north of the park tablet for Hindman's division near the railroad tracks.

Modern View of Bloody Pond

Bloody Pond, viewed here from the surrounding dense thickets on the southwest border of the park, is little more than a grassy depression, or sinkhole, except in periods of heavy rain, and is located on the east side of Lytle Road along the former route of the Dry Valley road. Buell's brigade and Sheridan's division retreated from the field of battle in a westerly direction, crossing the long north-south ridge partly visible in the background of this view. Hindman's division pursued for a distance of three-quarters of a mile before turning back. A metal park tablet stands by the roadside, to the far left of center in this view, indicating where the left of Hindman's division crossed the east leg of the Dry Valley Road, coming under fire from the high ground opposite.

Early View of Bloody Pond

Years before the formal opening of Chickamauga battlefield park, a wooden painted sign nailed to a tree identified the site of Bloody Pond.[4] An early park fingerpost has been staked in front in this early photograph (ca. 1892). This open view to the east, revealing a stretch of the Glenn-Kelly Road along the base of the distant trees, is now blocked by dense wooded thickets. The Glenn-Kelly Road skirts the base of Lytle Hill, just out of view to the left of this photograph.

Inscription at Bloody Pond

This illustrated park sign with a literary inscription previously stood (ca. 1980s) at the west end of the trail from the Glenn-Viniard Road to the site of Bloody Pond. This sign has been removed, and the trail to the site is unmarked; access is available via Lytle Road, along the general route of the old Dry Valley Road.

Confederate Breakthrough into South Dyer Field

At 11:20 A.M. on September 20, Major General Thomas Hindman's three infantry brigades moved forward in tandem on the left of Brigadier General Bushrod Johnson's division of Lieutenant General James Longstreet's wing. In his advance to the south of Brotherton field on Johnson's immediate left, Brigadier General Zachariah C. Deas's brigade crossed three hundred yards of dense forest with few or no skirmishers.[1] Startled Union skirmishers near the LaFayette Road ran to breastworks in the woods just to the west, where the decimated ranks of Colonel Carlin's brigade of Davis' Union division had just filed into position. Deas's infantry advanced in double-quick time and overwhelmed Carlin's thinly held line at the breastworks. With Bushrod Johnson pressing ahead on the right, both of Davis's Union brigades fled in disorder through the woods, and Deas's brigade broke into the south field of the Dyer farm at the site of the tanyard.[2]

Reacting in haste to the crisis, Major General Alexander M. McCook, commanding the remnants of the Union XX Army Corps, ordered a bayonet charge with the lead brigade (Laiboldt's) of Sheridan's division.[3] The rapidity of the Confederate advance, coupled with the incoming wave of Davis's routed soldiers, broke the momentum of Laiboldt's charge and increased the ranks of fleeing Union soldiers streaming back to the elevated ridge on the west side of the south Dyer field.[4] The timely arrival of Sheridan's next brigade in line, led by Brigadier General William H. Lytle, stalled Deas's advance when it reached the high ground at the south end of the ridge across Dyer field, striking the left flank Confederate units as they advanced up to and along the ridge. As Sheri-

dan later lamented, Lytle was killed in action as his brigade stubbornly resisted Deas's advance. Hindman's reserve brigade, led by Brigadier General Patton Anderson, moved up to fill the gap on Deas's left where Manigault had veered, and even the arrival and determined stand of Sheridan's third brigade, under the command of Colonel Walworth, failed to stem the concerted Confederate attack.[5]

By noon, Hindman had broken through the Union right, excepting Wilder's brigade to the south, with the remnants of Davis's and Sheridan's divisions racing across the Dry Valley road to the safety of the foothills to the west, past Rosecrans himself. The Union commander had witnessed the rout of his last hope for the right of his army and departed on the Dry Valley road with intentions, he later reported, of joining Thomas on the left. Evidence in the form of increasing numbers of fleeing Union troops reaching the escape route convinced the shaken army commander to continue on to McFarland's Gap en route to Chattanooga to consolidate a last stand there.[6]

DIRECTIONS: From Bloody Pond on Lytle Road, proceed north several hundred yards and turn right at the short roadway crossing back to the Chickamauga-Vittetoe Road. Turn right again and proceed approximately 0.75 mile to the intersection of the Glenn-Kelly Road. Turn left and continue a few hundred feet to the large open field and the sign on the left for the tanyard. Along the way, as an optional stop, visitors will pass the sign at the trail up the wooded hillside to the Lytle monument.

Modern View of Tanyard
in South Dyer Field

Below the ridge dividing south Dyer
field to the west, at the site of the tanyard, Stewart's attack on September 19
was turned back (a position marked by
the white park tablet), while Hindman's
breakthrough on the following day
proved unstoppable. The line of trees
perpendicular to the ridge on the far left
covers the slope of Lytle Hill. Monuments in the vicinity of the tablet mark
positions on the second day of battle
where Laibolt's bayonet charge began to
break up amid the confusion of Davis's
retreat from Deas's charging Confederates; the action occurred amid the ruins
of the Dyer tannery, an area of old logs
used for drying tanned leather and of
saltpeter (potash) beds.[7] At a critical
moment when Deas's brigade broke
through at the upper ridge line, forward
units of Lytle's brigade reached the hilltop located at the upper left of this view
and created a temporary setback there
by firing into the flank of Deas's lead
units until forced to withdraw by converging Confederate units.[8]

Modern View of Site
Where Lytle Fell

Little remains of the ten foot high py-
ramidal mound of cannonballs erected
at the site where Lytle fell on the second
day of battle at the climactic moment of
Hindman's attack. After leading the last
available infantry brigade of Sheridan's
division into close combat at the hilltop,
Lytle died at the site from multiple gunshot wounds as Confederate units
closed in from three sides. In this view,
looking northeast, the open grounds of
the tanyard, where the struggle to contain Hindman's breakthrough began,
are visible in the background. The line
of trees in the far distance borders the
Brotherton farm on the west. When
Lytle's brigade began forming on the
hilltop, dense smoke rose from burning
brush and grass in the field in front.
A Union soldier remembered: "Under
this [smoke] we could see, away down
the slope of the hill and across the
little valley just as far as the eye could
reach, moving masses of men hurrying
toward us."[9]

Unidentified View of Chickamauga Battlefield

A photograph from the Brady Studios collection of the National Archives captures a scene still only identified as a "Part of Chickamauga Battlefield." This view bears some resemblance to the low rise of ground at the south end of Dyer field where Lytle was killed, now known as Lytle Hill, although that hill is now and was wooded at the time of battle.[10] Similar sites existed as far north as Rossville Gap and west, along the route of Union retreat, across the network of foothills leading to Missionary Ridge. At the time Lytle was struck down in a crossfire of gunshots, Hindman's Confederate infantry were closing in on the hilltop position from three sides with overwhelming volleys of musketfire.[11]

Bushrod Johnson's Breakthrough into Dyer Field

Brigadier General Bushrod Johnson's infantry division of three brigades spearheaded the assault of Longstreet's wing at the Brotherton farm, with Hindman's division moving up on the immediate left. Johnson and Hindman scattered Jefferson Davis's two Union brigades from the recently vacated Union breastworks behind Brotherton field and emerged into the open field of the Dyer farm in line of battle. Union Brigadier General Wood's trailing brigade, under the command of Colonel Don Carlos Buell, was caught in column of march and driven back to the west after a brief struggle.

Some seven hundred yards directly west, Rosecrans viewed the disintegration of the center of his army from the elevated grounds of his latest headquarters and hurriedly rode south to coordinate resistance from the remnants of the Union right.[1] Bushrod Johnson apparently enjoyed his view from the Confederate perspective at the east wood line: "Our lines now emerged from the forest into open ground on the border of long, open fields, over which the enemy were retreating. . . . The scene now presented was unspeakably grand. The resolute and impetuous charge, the rush of our heavy columns sweeping out from the shadow and gloom of the forest. . . . Here, General Hood gave me the last order I received from him on the field, 'Go ahead, and keep ahead of everything.'"[2]

On Bushrod Johnson's right, McNair's brigade temporarily stalled in the face of stiff opposition from Brannan's two brigades at Poe farm, until Colonel Cyrus Sugg's reserve brigade and Brigadier General Henry "Rock" Benning's brigade of Hood's third line came up in support. Where Stewart's attack had failed earlier, Connell's Union brigade folded first, with his troops running back through the woods behind their position and through the stalled lines of Brigadier General Samuel Beatty's brigade of Van Cleve's division into the north Dyer field. As Beatty's command collapsed and his soldiers joined Connell's retreating ranks, Croxton's brigade also broke up in the Confederate onrush. Croxton was wounded and carried from the field as his command fragmented; some units withdrew north to the security of Reynolds's Kelly field line, while others joined in the hasty withdrawal west through Dyer field.[3]

Longstreet's attack had dispersed significant elements of five Union infantry divisions, including the whole of Davis's and Sheridan's, which led to the collapse of the Union right and center and the capture of large numbers of prisoners and cannon. Hindman followed in pursuit of Sheridan's routed division, while Bushrod Johnson and Hood turned their attention to a formidable line of cannon along the low ridge bordering the north Dyer field on the west. In the altered circumstances of battle, Longstreet's attack was now primarily directed north and northwest in pursuit of retreating Union units, abandoning the pivot to the left originally intended by Bragg.[4]

DIRECTIONS: From the site of the Tanyard, continue ahead to the pull-off at Tour Stop 7 to view the scene of Longstreet's breakthrough and the site of Rosecrans's last field headquarters from the perspective of the Battery G, Ohio Light Artillery monument.

From this tour stop there is also a convenient route to a site near the Vittetoe house (no longer standing): continue to the intersection of Dyer Road, turn left, and follow to the intersection with the Chickamauga-Vittetoe Road. Turn right, and proceed six hundred yards to the elevated cannon and marker at the site of York's battery, on the left. York's battery (commanded at Chickamauga by Lieutenant William S. Everett) fired past the site of the Vittetoe farm at Union units in retreat.

Dyer Field from the Tanyard

This photograph (ca. 1895), viewing north, reveals the open grounds of the Dyer farm from the site of the Tanyard, just south of the area where Bushrod Johnson witnessed the "unspeakably grand" scene at the time of the Confederate breakthrough. The park tablet in the center foreground indicates the point of deepest penetration of Clayton's brigade in the late afternoon of the first day of battle. The LaFayette Road follows a course roughly parallel to the woods on the far right, at a distance of four hundred to five hundred yards farther to the east. Stewart's infantry on the 19th and Longstreet's more powerful infantry force on the 20th both had to traverse this stretch of woods before emerging into the open Dyer field. In the center left of this view, a flagpole stands beside the postwar Dyer house, the first park headquarters. A shell monument at the site of Longstreet's field headquarters is located in the small grove of trees to the right of the Dyer house. In the far background, the observation tower marks the highest point of Snodgrass Hill.

Modern View of Dyer Field

The Battery G, First Ohio Light Artillery monument stands at the far right of center of this view and commemorates a battery withdrawn prior to Longstreet's breakthrough.[5] It is a prominent visual landmark for viewing the elevated rise of ground some four hundred yards directly to the west, out of view in this photograph, where Rosecrans's headquarters was located at the time of Longstreet's attack.

To the left center, the white outline of a park administration building identifies the original site of the Dyer house. No trace remains of the iron and steel observation tower on Snodgrass Hill, although a very distant view of those (now) tree-covered heights is still discernible in this modern view. The view of the ridge at the far end of the north Dyer field, where Harker's brigade delayed Longstreet's advance, is framed by the gap in the line of trees in the middle distance immediately to the left of the foreground park tablet.

Veterans of Chickamauga at the Dyer House

The Dyer house, in a central location of the battlefield west of the LaFayette Road, became the first park headquarters, even before the official opening in 1895. In this photograph (ca. 1892), two of the opposing field officers prominent in the fighting at Chickamauga stand side by side on the porch, just to the left of the front door: U.S. General John T. Wilder, formerly a colonel in the Union Army of the Cumberland, and Confederate General Alexander P. Stewart of the Army of Tennessee. The original house of John Dyer, his wife, and five children was destroyed by fire sometime during or immediately after the battle. The house seen in this photograph was constructed in the postwar years. Today, a park administration building stands near the site.

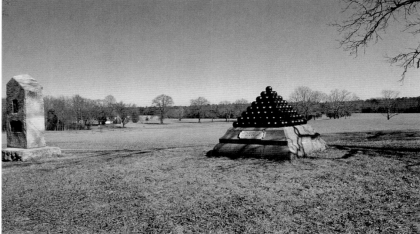

Aerial View of Rosecrans's Headquarters in South Dyer Field

The site of Rosecrans's headquarters near the southwest corner of Dyer field is marked by a pyramid of cannonballs near the isolated grouping of large trees just to the left of center in this photograph, looking northwest. At the foot of the heights immediately west, a thin line of woods masks the north-south route of an eastern leg of the old, long vanished Dry Valley road. Rosecrans departed the field of battle on this road, where "Fugitives, wounded, caissons, escort, ambulances, thronged the narrow pathways [to McFarland's Gap and on to Chattanooga]."[6] Other units, including Sheridan's division under close pursuit by Hindman's division, crossed over the rugged hills in a westerly direction. This route intersected with the western leg of the Dry Valley road that ran north along the base of Missionary Ridge. Missionary Ridge is visible in the distant background of this view, with the much larger line of Lookout Mountain looming in the far background.

General Rosecrans's Headquarters at the Time of Longstreet's Breakthrough

A shell monument and a larger stone monument to the Fifteenth Pennsylvania Cavalry Escort identify the site of Rosecrans's field headquarters on elevated ground overlooking the grounds of a long-vanished peach orchard, where the Union commander witnessed the spectacle of the retreating Union infantry at the time of Longstreet's breakthrough. Charles A. Dana, President Abraham Lincoln's assistant secretary of war, on temporary assignment to the Army of the Cumberland, awoke from a nap at the previously peaceful site: "I saw our lines break and melt away like leaves before the wind."[7] Bushrod Johnson described the open grounds north of the Dyer's peach orchard as a "stubble-field."[8]

North Dyer Field

Lieutenant General James Longstreet's forces continued to score successes in the area of north Dyer field that widened the scope of the breakthrough, despite several punishing setbacks. After completing the dispersal of Connell's and Croxton's Union brigades, Benning suffered what he initially viewed as a complete rout of his brigade in the corridor of woodland running north from the Poe farm. Major General Joseph Reynolds had reacted to the threat nearing his main line of defense south of Kelly field by hurriedly dispatching troops in a bayonet charge that caught Benning's soldiers on the right flank completely by surprise. Benning withdrew his command to the line of captured cannon in the vicinity of Poe farm.[1]

Offsetting the effective loss of Benning's brigade for offensive operations throughout the afternoon, combined Confederate operations were highly successful against a formidable line of Union artillery overlooking Confederate approaches through the north Dyer field. Twenty-nine cannon of various Union artillery units had been hastily assembled on the low ridge running along the western border of the Dyer field just before and during the time of the initial Confederate breakthrough. Major John Mendenhall, Chief of Artillery for Crittenden's XXI Corps, had earlier been assigned field command of the batteries. He failed to accumulate any significant infantry support as routed Union soldiers passed through the line of guns in their retreat. Mendenhall's massed artillery at Stone's River on January 2, 1863, had wrecked Breckinridge's division and altered the course of that battle. At Chickamauga, Mendenhall's plans were ruined by the rapid advance of Bushrod Johnson's and John Bell Hood's infantry and the weak Union infantry support. At least nine of the assembled cannon were captured in the onrush, while the rest were withdrawn in a hasty retreat to the Dry Valley road.[2]

At the north end of the open Dyer field, two isolated Union batteries continued to fire into the Confederate right flank from the top of a commanding rise of open ground. In the advance on Mendenhall's line of guns to the west, part of Brigadier General McIver Law's infantry division had changed front to capture these guns, exposing his right flank while awaiting reinforcements. Union Brigadier General Thomas Wood observed the movement from a location near the northeast corner of the field and directed his lead brigade, under the command of Colonel Charles Harker, to turn back and attack the Confederate flank. With Colonel Emerson Opdycke's 125th Ohio regiment leading the way with a bayonet charge, Harker's counterattack forced both Robertson's and Colonel James Sheffield's brigades of Law's division back several hundred yards through Dyer field to the shelter of projecting woods narrowing the field at the lower end.[3]

Hood was shot down with a crippling leg wound while attempting to rally Law's troops at the line of woods. Longstreet's depth of support in his wing command again proved crucial as Major General Joseph Kershaw's infantry division arrived at the scene in line of battle facing west only moments before Hood fell; at Hood's direction, Kershaw changed front to the right, stepping through the lines of Law's disorganized troops to counterattack north. Kershaw led his own brigade of South Carolinians directly forward towards Harker's line at the north end of Dyer field, with Brigadier General Benjamin G. Humphrey's brigade on the right and part of Bushrod Johnson's division on the left.

Kershaw's advancing troops were clothed in newly issued blue-dyed uniforms, which confused many Union officers, who waited too long before ordering firing to commence; Harker's front-line troops were overwhelmed by the converging Confederate units. Harker's retreat to the northwest crossed a ravine in front of the upper heights of Snodgrass Hill that would later provide a haven for Confederate infantry.[4] The fallback ended on an adjoining low ridge extending northeast from the Snodgrass cabin, where Harker joined a gathering patchwork of scattered Union units that were being organized by Brigadier General John M. Brannan for a last stand. Brannan had led scattered units from his own command at the Poe farm to this commanding elevation.[5]

Harker's stand at the north end of Dyer field had provided Brannan the critical time needed to organize a defensible line of battle. While Kershaw's infantry advanced in pursuit of Harker, Bushrod Johnson's division moved up to the line of the Dry Valley road, Longstreet ordered Hindman to return, and the climactic phase of the battle of Chickamauga began.

DIRECTIONS: From Tour Stop 7, proceed north on the Glenn-Kelly Road approximately 0.2 mile, just past the shell monument on the right at the site of Longstreet's corps headquarters, to the sign on the left pointing to the "Site Where Hood Was Wounded." The large open area just beyond is north Dyer field.

North Dyer Field

From a position along the Glenn-Kelly Road, viewing northwest across Dyer field, monuments along the upper heights of the ridge directly west identify the location where three Confederate brigades broke through Mendenhall's improvised line of twenty-nine cannon, capturing nine. To the right of this view, the tall South Carolina Confederate monument stands prominently atop the cleared ridge overlooking Harker's line of battle across the north end of Dyer field. Robertson's and Sheffield's brigades were forced to withdraw under intense musket fire to the line of woods several hundred yards to the south. Hood was wounded while rallying these troops and ordering Kershaw's and Humphrey's recently arrived brigades forward. Kershaw's brigade of six South Carolina regiments and Humphrey's Mississippi brigade succeeded in driving Harker's brigade back to the northwest, to the higher ground of Snodgrass Hill.

The Wounding of General Hood

An illustration by Civil War artist Frank Vizetelly depicts the scene when Major General John Bell Hood was wounded at a critical moment in the battle of Chickamauga. Field commander of three infantry divisions in Longstreet's wing during the breakthrough into north Dyer field, Hood was shot while coordinating troop deployment in the face of stiff opposition on the high ground to the north. Vizetelly's drawing reflects the historical setting in a stretch of woods jutting west into the Dyer field, where routed Confederate troops of Law's brigade regrouped, and Kershaw's division advanced in a counterattack.

Snodgrass Hill—Opening Moves

Brigadier General John Brannan initially supervised the organization of scattered units of the Union right and center as they arrived at the high ground of the Snodgrass farm in the wake of Lieutenant General James Longstreet's breakthrough. In the opening phase of combat, fewer than half of the Union forces who would later arrive to fight were present to defend more than half a mile of interconnected craggy heights that marked the easternmost extension of a fragmented spur of Missionary Ridge.[1] This heavily timbered range of peaks rising from the lower grounds of the Snodgrass fields and angling west comprised four major heights separated by ravines, described as "bastion-like spurs" by one Confederate officer.[2] To the west, Horseshoe Ridge, as it later became known, terminated in a sharp drop to the Dry Valley road near the site of the Vittetoe farm. Insufficient manpower at the onset of Confederate attacks forced Brannan to virtually concede the last, lower rise of ground to the west above the Vittetoe house, opening the way to a rear flank assault that Bushrod Johnson would later exploit.

By the hour of 1:00 P.M., with Harker's incoming brigade deployed on the left of Brannan's improvised line, Major General George Thomas arrived to assume command. Rosecrans and the other two corps commanders of the army had departed earlier for Chattanooga, leaving Thomas as the ranking officer on the field.[3]

Four Union infantry divisions remained in place at the Kelly farm at a time of quiet regrouping following Leonidas Polk's second failed attempt to attack down the LaFayette Road. An intervening five hundred yards of dense woods separated Thomas's dual command. Longstreet never exploited this gap as the battle developed, and, later in the afternoon, failed to detect Van Derveer's brigade and other units from the Kelly farm line as they cautiously approached through the woods to reinforce Thomas on the upper heights.[4]

Confederate attacks on Thomas's new position at the Snodgrass farm began almost immediately after his arrival. Kershaw's brigade attacked on a broad front from the southeast in the pursuit of Harker's withdrawing troops, first coming under heavy musket and artillery fire from the Union troops on top of the hill directly above the Snodgrass cabin (usually referred to as Snodgrass Hill).[5]

On Kershaw's far right, Brigadier General Benjamin G. Humphreys withdrew his brigade after engaging and inspecting the long, open field approach to Harker's new, elevated position below the Snodgrass cabin.[6] As if confirming Humphrey's discretion, Harker handily stopped Kershaw's right regiments with an innovative use of the terrain and concentrated artillery and volley fire. This first Confederate attack actually proved more successful in frontal assaults up the precipitous slopes of the hilltops, and some Confederate units planted their regimental flags within the hastily constructed log and rail breastworks on top.[7] With the Union lines stretched thin on the high ground, the chances for Confederate success and a calamitous Union defeat on Horseshoe Ridge would hinge on the determination of Union soldiers earlier driven back in disorderly retreat and the timely arrival of fresh reinforcements.

DIRECTIONS: From the area of north Dyer field, continue along the marked park route towards Tour Stop 8, turning left where indicated. Park in the pull-off in front of the Snodgrass cabin.

Modern View of Snodgrass Cabin

The restored Snodgrass cabin stands midway up the hill that bears the same name, the upper heights connecting to a grouping of broken spurs of Missionary Ridge that became known as Horseshoe Ridge. In this modern view from a position of Battery I, Fourth U.S. Artillery, in front of the cabin, the road turns sharply, ascending the hill where large numbers of monuments and markers identify more of the improvised line of battle first formed by Brannan from scattered units of the Union right and center. When Thomas arrived at the scene, he established field headquarters behind the Snodgrass house, at the base of the elevated ground defended by Harker's brigade. The Snodgrass house became a Union field hospital, where surgeons operated in the uproar of battle with cannon firing within a few steps of the doorway.

Snodgrass House in the 1890s

In 1855, George Washington Snodgrass purchased the land where Thomas would later earn the title the "Rock of Chickamauga." The log cabin in this photograph dates to 1848. In this view (ca. 1895), the Snodgrass farmstead remained little changed from descriptions of its 1863 appearance. At the opening of the battle, George Snodgrass and family remained within the cabin bounded by a shed, attached kitchen, and outer smokehouse. They remained there until the afternoon of the nineteenth, when the approaching battle, signaled by minié balls crashing through the roof, forced his family, along with many other locals, to move to the shelter of a ravine some distance to the northwest. In the aftermath, the Snodgrass family found their home a "shambles," stained with the blood and remains of amputations by first Union and later Confederate surgeons.[8]

Position of Harker's Brigade below Snodgrass Barn

Brigadier General Thomas Wood, commanding Harker's brigade of his own division on the high ground at the Snodgrass farm, found his position a "natural parapet" where sustained volleys of musket fire could be delivered with minimal casualties. Lacking time and materials to construct protective defenses, "The regiments were advanced to the crest of the ridge alternately, and delivered their fire by volley at the command, retiring a few paces . . . to reload."[9] In the foreground of this photograph (ca. 1895) where monuments and markers indicate Harker's position, two cannon flank the monument to the Eighteenth Ohio Light Artillery representing a late-arriving battery of Granger's reserve corps posted, by Thomas's order, to support Harker's line of battle six hundred feet northeast of the Snodgrass house. Some modern historical scholarship concludes that the markers for Union positions at the Snodgrass farm and Horseshoe Ridge are misplaced. Historian William Glenn Robertson suggests that "most Federal markers should be shifted approximately one brigade front to the west."[10]

Tennessee Artillery Monument—Forrest's Defense and Granger's Approach

Through the early morning hours of September 20, Forrest's cavalry participated in reconnaissance and skirmishing missions guarding the right of Polk's wing command. Forrest deployed his artillery and both of his cavalry divisions along the open crest of a low ridge running north across Reed's Bridge Road some seven hundred yards east of the LaFayette Road.

In mid-morning, Forrest advanced his cavalry across the LaFayette Road and captured the Union field hospital near Cloud Springs, approximately one half mile north of the McDonald farm. Within two hours, Forrest's cavalry had abandoned the hospital in preliminary skirmishing with the advance of Steedman's division of Granger's reserve corps and withdrawn to the prepared line of artillery on the ridge east of the LaFayette Road. Davidson's dismounted brigade of cavalry was posted in an open field below the guns.

Forrest unleashed barrages of shell fire that forced Granger to deploy in line of battle. For a critical length of time, when events of momentous significance would hinge on the duration of Forrest's delaying action, Granger prepared to attack, advancing his own artillery to the roadside and preparing the infantry for a charge. At the last moment before ordering a charge, Granger sensed the lack of infantry support in Forrest's opposing line and diverted Steedman's two brigades southwest, to the rising uproar of battle across the McDonald and Mullis fields, on the heights of Snodgrass Hill. Granger ordered Colonel Daniel McCook's brigade down from the vicinity of McAfee's Church to confront and contain Forrest's cavalry.[1]

DIRECTIONS: The site of the Tennessee Artillery monument on Reed's Bridge Road is located approximately 0.4 mile east of the LaFayette Road. This site of Forrest's and Granger's confrontation on the second day of battle may be conveniently reserved for inspection after returning to the Visitor Center from Snodgrass Hill.

Tennessee Artillery Monument

Along Reed's Bridge Road, at a distance of some seven hundred yards east of U.S. Highway 27, the Tennessee Artillery monument stands on the crest of a low ridge that in 1863 overlooked with a clear view the LaFayette Road approaches to the Confederate right flank on the second day of battle. Heavy regrowth of trees now obscures most of the view back to the west from the site, near the south end of a line of fifteen cannon assembled by Forrest. A small stone block to the immediate left of the three park tablets across the road marks a position on the line of the three Tennessee batteries of Forrest's cavalry.

Reenactors Portray Morton's Battery of Forrest's Artillery

Confederate artillery batteries were generally organized into units smaller than their Union counterparts, with four, rather than six, cannon and a manpower limit of eighty personnel rather than the Union limit of 156. In the field, each gun could be operated with a nine-man crew firing as often as twice per minute.[2] Forrest deployed fifteen cannon on the low ridge some seven hundred yards east of the LaFayette Road in his final effort to impede Granger's Union infantry on September 20. Steedman of Granger's reserve corps reported his infantry had been shelled by Confederate batteries for a distance of two miles on their approach. Captain John W. Morton Jr.'s, Captain A. L. Huggins's, and Huwald's Tennessee batteries of Forrest's cavalry corps were supplemented by a section of Captain Robert Cobb's Kentucky battery from Major General John C. Breckinridge's division.[3]

Horseshoe Ridge—the Climactic Struggle

Brigadier General Kershaw's first attack on the Snodgrass heights failed to break through, despite temporary breaches at the top. On the flanks of the overextended front, little progress had been made against Harker's new line, on Thomas's far left, and the line of the Twenty-first Ohio Regiment, armed with Colt revolving-cylinder repeating rifles, anchoring Union lines to the west.

On the heights directly above the Snodgrass cabin, some Confederates broke through at the top, only to be confronted with incoming Union reinforcements. Colonel Timothy Stanley, with the driven remnants of his brigade, arrived at an opportune moment and charged past the Fourth U.S. Artillery Battery to force the Confederates off Snodgrass Hill, the first remarkably timed arrival of Union reinforcements that would help forestall Union defeat throughout the afternoon.[1] Stanley fell wounded in the fighting and was succeeded in command by Colonel William L. Stoughton.

As Kershaw's units re-formed in the cover of log and rail breastworks at the low ground below Horseshoe Ridge and fended off sporadic counterattacks, two brigades of Bushrod Johnson's division arrived at the site of the Vittetoe house and began climbing the undefended heights east of the Dry Valley road. Near the hour of 2:00 P.M., at the western outpost of Union lines on Horseshoe Ridge, with Patton Anderson's brigade of Hindman's division pinning down the main force of the Twenty-first Ohio in frontal attacks from the south, Bushrod Johnson's troops were poised for a sweep across the thin line of soldiers guarding the Union upper right flank.

At a moment of pending calamity for the Horseshoe Ridge defenders, with Kershaw's troops again moving forward in support, four thousand fresh Union infantry of Brigadier General James B. Steedman's division of Granger's reserve corps unexpectedly appeared on the rear slopes below the approaching

Confederates. Steedman's infantry had deployed on the run to the threatened right flank, advancing up the back slopes to engage in a bitterly fought battle of attack and counterattack that would temporarily secure the Union lines on the right, at a cost of nearly a thousand men in Steedman's division in a space of time he estimated as twenty minutes. Military legends were born with the timing and importance of Granger's forced march, without direct orders, from the vicinity of Rossville to the aid of Thomas's lines on Horseshoe Ridge. In a brief lull, Bushrod Johnson prepared to renew fighting with the late-arriving troops of Hindman's other two brigades.[2]

The "Rock of Chickamauga," as Thomas would become known, managed to hold the Snodgrass heights through several more hours of sustained and increasingly coordinated Confederate attacks. Two more Union infantry brigades, including Van Derveer's and Hazen's, arrived from the relatively quiet Kelly field position.[3]

Following a meeting with the Confederate commander, at which General Braxton Bragg rejected his request for reinforcements from Polk's battered command, Longstreet belatedly moved to coordinate the attacks of his wing command. Bragg only hinted of concerted army operations with the statement that he was preparing to move his headquarters north, to the vicinity of Jay's Mill, closer to Polk's stalled wing command.

Longstreet returned to his headquarters near the Dyer house and intensified direct command coordination, a deficiency in the Confederate left wing since the wounding of General Hood. Preston's reserve division was called in, and the final series of combined Confederate operations on the Snodgrass heights began before the hour of 4:00 P.M. While Humphrey's brigade remained inactive, along with Law's and Alexander P. Stewart's divisions, Kershaw's brigade, with the divisions of Hindman, Bushrod Johnson, and, finally, Preston, was hurled into the fight against the nearly intact Union divisions of Steedman and Brannan, with components of Wood's, Negley's, and Van Cleve's.[4]

Major General William Rosecrans, from new headquarters in Chattanooga, dispatched orders to Thomas in the late afternoon for a complete withdrawal of all forces in the field. As a part of Brigadier General Archibald Gracie Jr.'s brigade of Preston's division succeeded in occupying the hilltop directly above the Snodgrass cabin, Thomas began the pullback with the four divisions at the Kelly farm position, coincidentally at a time when Polk's wing had finally launched the long-delayed coordinated offensive Bragg desperately sought. Confederate attacks interrupted the planned orderly withdrawal of Union troops from Kelly field, and heavy losses were incurred, although the shock of Turchin's bayonet charge through Liddell's advance lines in McDonald field secured the western route of retreat to McFarland's Gap.

At Horseshoe Ridge, ammunition for both sides became a critical issue. The bodies of dead and wounded soldiers were scavenged to continue the fight. As guns jammed with overuse and cartridge boxes were emptied, Union units were increasingly forced to employ bayonet charges to hold on.

As darkness shrouded the slopes of Horseshoe Ridge, nearly all of the remaining Union forces were in retreat along the general route of McFarland's Gap Road, through the nearby foothills of Missionary Ridge. Portions of three Union regiments, inadvertently left behind, were captured as Longstreet's infantry closed in on the hilltops in near total darkness, ending the battle.[5]

DIRECTIONS: Monuments and markers related to the struggle on Horseshoe Ridge line the trail leading west from the site of Tour Stop 8 on top of Snodgrass Hill. An alternative route, from the Confederate perspective, leads from the Vittetoe Trail that branches left along the roadway leading to the Snodgrass cabin. This alternative route, which still leads to the area where the Vittetoe house once stood, passes a branching trail down to the site of the South Carolina monument, overlooking the scene of action in north Dyer field.

Part of the Union Line of Battle atop Snodgrass Hill

One of the more visually inspiring regimental monuments on the battlefield stands in the foreground of this view of monuments along the upper heights directly above the Snodgrass cabin, at the designated junction of Stanley's and Brannan's lines of battle. The Second Minnesota infantry monument, mounted with figures of three soldiers, one bearing a flag, is situated below the upper hilltop position where this regiment of Van Derveer's brigade actually fought. Monuments marking positions of Stanley's (Stoughton's) brigade and other units, in the left background, stand along the crest of steep slopes where Union soldiers fought behind the additional protection of hastily erected fieldworks of rails, trees, and rocks. These breastworks, and the cannon batteries in close support, controlled approaches through north Dyer field and the lower ground in front of the slopes, where Kershaw's, and later Preston's, infantry was formed for assault.

Observation Tower on Snodgrass Hill

One of the three observation towers erected on the battlefield when the park opened stood at the highest point of Horseshoe Ridge, on the second rise of ground above the Snodgrass cabin. With a height of seventy feet to the upper platform, each of these towers, in full view of each other, provided unobstructed views in all directions to facilitate the study of campaign strategy and tactical movements. This tower stands in the background of the Thirty-fifth Ohio regimental monument, a unit of Van Derveer's brigade under the command of Colonel Henry Boynton. Reported losses in this regiment totaled nearly 50 percent, accumulated in actions during the opening of the battle above Jay's Mill, the repulse of Stovall's brigade in Kelly field, and the hours of desperate struggle on these heights.[6] The Snodgrass tower remained as the last of the five originals (two others were located on Missionary Ridge with a view of the battlefield) until 1947, when it was dismantled and removed for use elsewhere.[7]

View of Granger's Approach to Snodgrass Hill

This photograph (ca. 1928), looking northeast from Snodgrass Hill, possibly from the iron and steel observation tower, provides a panoramic view of the open grounds crossed by the infantry of Granger's reserve corps in their approach to Snodgrass Hill. Steedman's two brigades, diverted southwest by Forrest's stand east of the LaFayette Road, marched through the open fields of the McDonald, Mullis, and Snodgrass farms to reach Thomas's embattled position. The buildings and grounds of Fort Oglethorpe, established in 1902, lie to the distant north, at the upper left of this view. The next open field to the north of the Snodgrass farm, reaching to the distant south boundary line of Fort Oglethorpe in this view, belonged to the Mullis family. Steedman's infantry, as they approached the Snodgrass farm, raised clouds of dust in their march through the parched Mullis cornfield. The open view that Thomas observed at the time of the battle from the lower grounds of the Snodgrass farm across the Mullis fields would have been compromised by the time of this 1928 view by the encroaching growth of trees in the middle distance. Trees now cover nearly all of the grounds of the Mullis farm. The Snodgrass cabin and monuments marking the positions of Harker and Hazen are visible at the lower right of this view.

View of Horseshoe Ridge Where "Lost Regiments" Were Captured

This photograph (ca. 1895) provides a rare open view to the west of the ground along Horseshoe Ridge near positions at the right of Brannan's line of battle and the left of Steedman's. The large monument at right center marks a position of Brannan's Twenty-first Ohio in the low depression between the second and third hills of Horseshoe Ridge. Armed with five-shot Colt repeating rifles and fighting desperately with dwindling ammunition against Bushrod Johnson's flanking attack, this regiment and all of the outstretched Union lines on Horse-shoe Ridge teetered on the verge of collapse just as Steedman's charge changed the course of the battle. Just left of center, at the hilltop, is the monument to the Twenty-second Michigan, which anchored the left flank of Steedman's division after the repulse of Bushrod Johnson's initial attack. These regiments were two of the three left behind in the late afternoon pullout; they were surprised and captured in gathering darkness on this ground.[8] These monuments, as previously mentioned, were presumably placed farther east than the corresponding units' original positions.

Ground of Kershaw's and Gracie's Assault on Stanley's Brigade, Snodgrass Hill

In the late afternoon of September 20, during the major coordinated assault by nine brigades of Longstreet's infantry, part of Brigadier General Archibald Gracie's brigade of Preston's division attacked the position of Stoughton's brigade along the crest of this sloping ground directly above the Snodgrass house. As Gracie later reported: "Passing through Kershaw's command, the brigade found . . . the enemy strongly posted behind breastworks of logs and rails on the crest of an opposite hill. . . . [T]he brigade scaled the precipitous heights, driving the enemy before it, and took possession of the hill."[9] Kershaw's and Gracie's troops launched their attacks from their own hastily built field-works in a ravine at the base of these heights, crossing the Vittetoe Road for the final assault to the top. The Vittetoe Road (trail) still leads to the site where the Vittetoe house stood, at the base of the southernmost hill of Horseshoe Ridge.

Vittetoe House

The Vittetoe house stands in the staging area where Hindman and Bushrod Johnson launched their assaults on the extreme right of Union defenses on Horseshoe Ridge; it is the smaller cabin just left of center in this photograph (ca. 1895) that looks northwest from a position west of the Crawfish Springs Road. The house is located at the foot of the western limit of Horseshoe Ridge, just south of a narrow gap in the foothills leading to McFarland's Gap. A line of telegraph wires that had connected Rosecrans's headquarters at the Widow Glenn's to Chattanooga and on to Washington during the battle extended along the route of the Dry Valley road. Bushrod Johnson captured a train of Union wagons, caissons, and a battery of artillery stalled in the chaotic congestion of retreat at the narrow gap near the Vittetoe house.[10]

Close-up of the Vittetoe House

This view of the Vittetoe house (ca. 1895) from the west reveals the line of approach of Bushrod Johnson's division from the low ridge to the right and the line of attack on Horseshoe Ridge to the left. Sugg's and Fulton's brigades advanced to the heights along the route of the Vittetoe Road, shown intersecting the Crawfish Springs Road at the left background of this view. This was the near-breakthrough flank attack that collapsed in the shock of Steedman's charge. When Bushrod Johnson first arrived at the Vittetoe house, he found a number of wounded Union soldiers and the grateful family of Hiram Vittetoe. "The ladies . . . who had taken shelter from danger on Saturday and Sunday beneath the floor now burst forth and greeted our soldiers with clapping of hands and shouts of joy."[11]

Route of Union Retreat through Gap near Vittetoe House

This postcard view of the gap through the spurs of Missionary Ridge just north of the site of the Vittetoe house is now completely blocked by heavy growth of trees and bushes. The imprinted title is partially correct, as the road through this gorge, along the route of Union retreat, does lead to McFarland's Gap two miles to the northwest. Bushrod Johnson captured a train of wagons, caissons, and guns at the gorge by directing Lieutenant W. S. Everett's Georgia battery (originally York's) to open fire, creating the "utmost consternation . . . causing some of the wagons to be upset and others to be run against trees."[12]

1509. McFarland's Gap. near Chickamauga Battlefield.

Kelly Farm to McFarland's Gap—Closing of the Battle

After several hours of battling Thomas's fortified and heavily reinforced lines at the Kelly farm, Polk's battered right wing command remained inactive for much of the afternoon. Cheatham's division arrived at the front, and Forrest's cavalry fought on the far right with Granger's Union reserve corps as it approached from Rossville.[1]

By the hour of 4:30 P.M., Polk had finally launched a coordinated assault of his wing command coincidentally at about the same time Thomas had ordered a withdrawal of the four Union infantry divisions remaining at the Kelly farm line. Confederate artillery was pushed to the front, and, despite strong resistance and punishing fire, Polk's infantry broke through the formidable line of Union breastworks. Elated troops leaped over the barricades and captured a number of prisoners from the retreating units of the Union left. The troops' emotional outburst as the advance of Polk's right wing command met forces of Lieutenant General James Longstreet's left wing command advancing north from Poe farm positions is described by D. H. Hill: "The cheers that went up when the two wings met were such as I had never heard before, and shall never hear again."[2]

At the site of his new headquarters near Jay's Mill, Bragg remained isolated from the excitement at the distant front lines while brooding over the earlier miscues and failures of Polk's command that, in his view, doomed his plan of a complete victory. As if in confirmation of Bragg's gloom, an impetuous charge by Turchin's brigade of Reynolds's Union division drove back forward units of Brigadier General St. John Liddell's Confederate infantry division from the upper grounds of the McDonald Farm and secured the route of McFarland's Gap Road for the safe retreat of the remaining units of the Union army.[3]

Liddell's Batteries at McDonald Farm at Closing of Battle

Snodgrass Hill rises in the distant left background of this turn-of-the-century photograph viewing to the southwest. The cannon represent Warren's Mississippi light artillery and Fowler's Alabama batteries of Liddell's infantry division, as they were positioned on the high ground just northwest of the site of the McDonald house. This Confederate artillery was aimed at the rise of ground several hundred yards to the northwest, where Union cannon of Dan McCook's brigade enfiladed the advance of Liddell's infantry through the McDonald and Mullis fields in the closing hours of battle.

McFarland's Gap through Missionary Ridge

Looking south from an upper shoulder of McFarland's Gap, the downhill route of Mission Ridge Road, following the route of the old Dry Valley road, still intersects the east-west route of McFarland's Gap Road at the narrow gap through Missionary Ridge. Here, on September 20, 1863, the chaotic scene included disorganized troops in full retreat, with ambulances, caissons, and ammunition wagons choking the pass. As a result of massive landscape alterations for modern highway construction, the route and setting of McFarland's Gap past this intersection, driving west, are radically different from the approach to the open fields of the McFarland farm where Generals Negley and Davis collected and organized the scattered fragments of Union infantry for Confederate attacks that failed to materialize.

The Battle of Chickamauga ended in a Confederate victory whose merits have been debated since the last shots were fired. General Braxton Bragg's Army of Tennessee, with the particularly outstanding contributions of Lieutenant General James Longstreet's command, had wrecked the Georgia offensive of the Union Army of the Cumberland, driving the demoralized fragments into the temporary safety of the old Confederate fieldworks surrounding Chattanooga. Significant numbers of prisoners, guns, cannon, and matériel were captured, although most of the Union supply wagons arrived intact in Chattanooga.

The cost was staggering for both armies. Union losses totaling more than sixteen thousand killed, wounded, or missing included thousands of wounded soldiers left on the battlefield and in captured field hospitals. Confederate losses were even more severe, totaling more than eighteen thousand.[1] In Bragg's view, a heavy toll of dead horses compounded the situation for the Confederates,

crippling already marginal transport capabilities for further offensive operations. Bragg did not act on Longstreet's suggestion of an offensive into Tennessee behind the Union army at Chattanooga, later expressing concerns about transportation and logistics.[2]

Bragg ignited a new and growing storm of bitter controversy within his own ranks of officers by failing to order a timely pursuit when not all of Rosecrans's army had concentrated within the inner defenses of Chattanooga. Bragg's army began moving up on the following day, and, by September 23, occupied the line of Missionary Ridge and Lookout Mountain in the onset of Confederate siege operations. Some twenty years later, D. H. Hill offered this epitaph to the battle of Chickamauga, referring to Longstreet's oft-quoted worst fear prior to leaving General Robert E. Lee's army en route to Georgia: "That 'barren victory' sealed the fate of the Southern Confederacy."[3]

ABBREVIATIONS

Boynton, *Chickamauga Guide*   Boynton, H. V. *The Chickamauga National Military Park: An Historical Guide, with Maps and Illustrations.*

Boynton, *Dedication*   Boynton, H. V. *Dedication of the Chickamauga and Chattanooga National Military Park, September 18–20, 1895.*

CCNMP   Chickamauga and Chattanooga National Military Park archives

LC   Library of Congress

NA   National Archives

O.R.   *War of the Rebellion: A Compilation of the Official Records of the Union and Confederate Armies,* Ser. 1.

USAMHI   United States Army Military History Institute

USGS   United States Geological Survey (Department of the Interior)

NOTES

Introduction

1. Boynton, *Dedication*, 43.
2. Boynton, *Chickamauga Guide*, 219.
3. Ibid., 219.
4. Paige and Greene, *Administrative History*.
5. Boynton, *Chickamauga Guide*, 219.
6. Trowbridge, *Picture of the Desolated States*, 264.

Gordon-Lee House

1. O.R., vol. 30, part 1, 54–55; Boynton, *Chickamauga Guide*, 169; Green, *Witness of a House*, 5.
2. Robertson et al., *Staff Ride Handbook*, 45.
3. Green, *Witness of a House*.
4. *Indiana at Chickamauga*, 301.

Lee and Gordon's Mill

1. O.R., vol. 30, part 2, 23–24, 28–31; O.R., vol. 30, part 1, 53–54, 629–30.
2. O.R., vol. 30, part 1, 54–56.
3. Ibid., part 2, 52.
4. Green, *Witness of a House*, 1–2.
5. Text of Georgia state historical marker at entrance to site.

John Ross House at Rossville Gap in Missionary Ridge

1. O.R., vol. 30, part 1, 853–54.
2. Ibid.
3. Moulton, *John Ross*, 9, 11.

Reed's Bridge

1. O.R., vol. 30, part 2, 31–32, 451–52, 467; O.R., vol. 30, part 1, 922–23.
2. Ibid., part 1, 923.

Alexander's Bridge

1. O.R., vol. 30, part 1, 447, 466; O.R., vol. 30, part 2, 251, 257, 271–72.
2. O.R., vol. 30, part 2, 503.
3. *Indiana at Chickamauga*, 205.
4. Ibid., 301.

McDonald Farm—Later Site of Visitor Center

1. O.R., vol. 30, part 1, 53–56, 248–49; O.R., vol. 30, part 2, 23–24.
2. Cozzens, *This Terrible Sound*, 144; O.R., vol. 30, part 1, 290.

McCook's Position on Reed's Bridge Road

1. O.R., vol. 30, part 1, 853–54, 871.
2. Ibid., 875; O.R., vol. 30, part 2, 528.
3. O.R., vol. 30, part 1, 249.
4. Ibid., 871; in Cozzens, *This Terrible Sound*, 122, there is contradictory evidence of the report.

Jay's Mill—Opening of the Battle

1. O.R., vol. 30, part 2, 32, 524, 527–29; O.R., vol. 30, part 1, 248–50, 440, 415–16.
2. O.R., vol. 30, part 2, 529.
3. Minnich, *Unique Experiences in the Chickamauga Campaign*, 381–84.
4. Boynton, *Chickamauga Guide*, xvi.
5. Ibid.
6. Ibid.

Vicinity of Wilson's Attack

1. O.R., vol. 30, part 1, 415–16; O.R., vol. 30, part 2, 248, 524.
2. Wilson, *Under the Old Flag*, 169.
3. O.R., vol. 30, part 1, 249–50, 275–76, 286–87, 400–401, 415–16; O.R., vol. 30, part 2, 248, 524.

4. O.R., vol. 30, part 2, 251; O.R., vol. 30, part 1, 534.

5. O.R., vol. 30, part 1, 248.

6. Ibid., 432.

7. Sorrell, *Recollections of a Confederate Staff Officer*, 183.

Winfrey Field

1. O.R., vol. 30, part 1, 249–50, 275–76, 400–401, 415–16; O.R., vol. 30, part 2, 248, 251–52, 272–73, 524; O.R., vol. 30, part 1, 293.

2. O.R., vol. 30, part 1, 275; Belknap, *History*, 170–71.

3. O.R., vol. 30, part 2, 271–73.

4. Ibid., 252, 273–74.

5. Belknap, *History*, 170–71.

6. O.R., vol. 30, part 2, 277–78.

Van Derveer's Position on Reed's Bridge Road

1. O.R., vol. 30, part 1, 427–29.

2. Minnich, *Unique Experiences in the Chickamauga Campaign*, 382; O.R., vol. 30, part 2, 524; O.R., vol. 30, part 1, 432–33; McElroy, *Chickamauga*, 7, 28–29, 56; O.R., vol. 30, part 1, 428–29, 432–33.

3. Boynton, *Chickamauga Guide*, 177.

4. Ibid., 4.

Preston Smith and Seventy-seventh Pennsylvania Monuments—Cleburne's Twilight Assault

1. O.R., vol. 30, part 1, 250–51.

2. Ibid., part 2, 153–54.

3. Ibid., 176; O.R., vol. 30, part 1, 287, 299–301.

4. O.R., vol. 30, part 2, 154.

5. Ibid., 107–8; Skinner, ed., *Pennsylvania at Chickamauga*, 197.

6. Skinner, ed., *Pennsylvania at Chickamauga*, 406.

Brock Field

1. O.R., vol. 30, part 1, 534–35.

2. Ibid., 713.

3. Ibid., 416; O.R., vol. 30, part 2, 78, 83–84.

4. O.R., vol. 30, part 1, 713.

5. Ibid., 761–62, 773; O.R., vol. 30, part 2, 106–7.

6. O.R., vol. 30, part 2, 94, 99.

7. Ibid., 126.

8. Ibid., 119; T. L. Massenburg, "Captain W. W. Carnes' Battery at Chickamauga," *Confederate Veteran* 8, no. 11 (Nov. 1898), 517–18.

Brotherton Farm

1. O.R., vol. 30, part 2, 361–62.

2. Boynton, *Chickamauga Guide*, 37; O.R., vol. 30, part 1, 383–84, 402, 473–74; O.R., vol. 30, part 2, 456, 762, 816.

3. O.R., vol. 30, part 1, 471, 836; O.R., vol. 30, part 2, 388–89.

Poe Field

1. O.R., vol. 30, part 1, 762, 799; O.R., vol. 30, part 2, 383–84, 397.

2. *The Collected Works of Ambrose Bierce*, 10 vols. (New York: Gordian Press, 1960), 1:271–72. Bierce's reminiscence of the fighting was originally published as "A Little of Chickamauga."

3. O.R., vol. 30, part 2, 384.

West Brock Field

1. O.R., vol. 30, part 1, 447.

2. Ibid., part 2, 32, 453–54, 510.

3. Ibid., 453–54, 473–74, 499–500; O.R., vol. 30, part 1, 56, 447–48, 529–30.

Viniard Farm

1. O.R., vol. 30, part 1, 498–99.

2. Cozzens, *This Terrible Sound*, 198.

3. O.R., vol. 30, part 1, 669.

4. Ibid., part 2, 32; Connelly, *Autumn of Glory*, 206.

5. O.R., vol. 30, part 2, 430–31, 453–56, 510–11, 517–18; O.R., vol. 30, part 1, 56–57, 447–48, 498–99, 515–16, 529–30, 599, 668–71.

6. Spruill, ed., *Guide to the Battle*, 83.

7. O.R., vol. 30, part 1, 529.

8. Ibid., part 2, 518.

9. Polley, *Hood's Texas Brigade*, 211–12.

10. Private communication with Gladys Dailey Nevels, whose father, W. F. Dailey, poses with the schoolchildren in the photograph.

11. *Indianapolis Daily Journal*, Sept. 28, 1863.

12. Eli Lilly and Company archives.

John Ingraham Grave—Interlude of Battle

1. Skinner, ed., *Pennsylvania at Chickamauga,* 128.
2. Thomas F. Berry, *Four Years with Morgan and Forrest* (Oklahoma City: Harlow-Ratliff Co., 1914), 243.
3. Connelly, *Autumn of Glory,* 207.
4. Longstreet, *From Manassas to Appomattox,* 437–38; O.R., vol. 30, part 2, 32–33.
5. O.R., vol. 30, part 2, 32.
6. Ibid., 32, 47.
7. Ibid., part 1, 57–58.
8. Robertson et al., *Staff Ride Handbook,* 74.
9. Watkins, *"Co. Aytch,"* 110. Reprinted with permission of Scribner, an imprint of Simon and Schuster Adult Publishing Group, from *"Co. Aytch": A Side Show of the Big Side Show,* by Sam R. Watkins (New York: Simon and Schuster, 1997).

McDonald Farm—Approaches to Kelly Field

1. O.R., vol. 30, part 2, 38, 47, 198; O.R., vol. 30, part 1, 277.
2. O.R., vol. 30, part 1, 251, 367–68.
3. Ibid., 251, 367, 277–78, 429–30, 379.
4. Ibid.; O.R., vol. 30, part 2, 141–42, 198–200, 253.
5. O.R., vol. 30, part 2, 229–30.
6. Boynton, *Chickamauga Guide,* xii.

Kelly Farm and Vicinity

1. Hill, "Chickamauga," 655–56; O.R., vol. 30, part 2, 198–99, 245–46; O.R., vol. 30, part 1, 277–78, 316.
2. O.R., vol. 30, part 2, 154.
3. Ibid., 154–56, 161–62, 176–77; O.R., vol. 30, part 1, 714, 763–64.
4. O.R., vol. 30, part 2, 60, 241, 363–64; O.R., vol. 30, part 1, 58–59.
5. Longstreet, *From Manassas to Appomattox,* 450–51.
6. O.R., vol. 30, part 2, 209.
7. Ibid., part 1, 310.
8. *Indiana at Chickamauga,* 285.
9. O.R., vol. 30, part 2, 155.
10. Ibid., part 1, 763.
11. McElroy, *Chickamauga,* 122.
12. O.R., vol. 30, part 1, 553; McKinney, *Education in Violence.*

Poe Farm

1. O.R., vol. 30, part 2, 162.
2. Ibid., part 1, 429.
3. Cozzens, *This Terrible Sound,* 360.
4. O.R., vol. 30, part 1, 58–59.
5. Ibid., 635.
6. Ibid., part 2, 288, 364.
7. Ibid., 169.
8. Ibid., 364.
9. Ibid., 161–62, 363–64, 385–86; O.R., vol. 30, part 1, 402, 409–10, 417–20.
10. Spruill, ed., *Guide to the Battle,* 155.
11. O.R., vol. 30, part 2, 363.
12. Ibid., 363, 390; Spruill, ed., *Guide to the Battle,* 162.

Brotherton Farm

1. O.R., vol. 30, part 2, 287–88.
2. Ibid., part 1, 634.
3. Ibid., 500.
4. Ibid., 500, 655; O.R., vol. 30, part 2, 456–57
5. O.R., vol. 30, part 1, 59.
6. Ibid., part 2, 457.
7. Ibid., 474.
8. Ibid., 465–66.
9. Robertson et al., *Staff Ride Handbook,* 115–16.
10. Hill, "Chickamauga," 663–64.

West Brock Field

1. O.R., vol. 30, part 2, 341.
2. *Indiana at Chickamauga,* 206.
3. O.R., vol. 30, part 2, 342.
4. Belknap, *History,* 136.

Widow Glenn's Farm

1. Tucker, *Chickamauga,* 138.
2. O.R., vol. 30, part 1, 57.
3. Ibid., 503.
4. Ibid., 57.
5. Ibid., 57–58.
6. Ibid., 448, 579–80, 583.

7. *Indiana at Chickamauga*, 206–7; O.R., vol. 30, part 2, 341–42, 346.

8. Cozzens, *This Terrible Sound*, 393.

9. *Indiana at Chickamauga*, 206.

10. Baumgartner, *Blue Lightning*, 199–200.

11. Belknap, *History*, 136.

12. L. W. Mulhane, *Memorial of Major-General William Starke Rosecrans* (Mount Vernon, Ohio, 1898), quoted in Robertson, *Staff Ride Handbook*, 123.

Bloody Pond

1. Connelly, *Autumn of Glory*, 207; Cozzens, *This Terrible Sound*, 281; Tucker, *Chickamauga*, 187; *Indiana at Chickamauga*, 181.

2. John T. Wilder, "Unpublished Supplement to Official Report," Nov. 25, 1888, CCNMP.

3. O.R., vol. 30, part 2, 287.

4. Painted wooden signs identifying battlefield sites at Chickamauga date to October 1863, on the occasion of a visit by Confederate President Jefferson Davis (unpublished diary in CCNMP archives, as described by James Ogden III, Chief Historian, CCNMP).

Confederate Breakthrough into South Dyer Field

1. O.R., vol. 30, part 2, 317, 352.

2. Ibid., 303, 329–30, 317, 333–34; O.R., vol. 30, part 1, 60, 530.

3. O.R., vol. 30, part 1, 590.

4. Ibid., 580, 590; O.R., vol. 30, part 2, 303.

5. O.R., vol. 30, part 1, 580; O.R., vol. 30, part 2, 303.

6. O.R., vol. 30, part 1, 59.

7. Belknap, *History*, 246.

8. Ibid., 136.

9. Bennett, *History of Thirty-sixth Regiment Illinois Volunteers*, 469.

10. O.R., vol. 30, part 2, 317.

11. Ibid., part 1, 595.

Bushrod Johnson's Breakthrough into Dyer Field

1. O.R., vol. 30, part 1, 59, 656.

2. Ibid., part 2, 457.

3. Ibid.; Robertson et al., *Staff Ride Handbook*, 118; O.R., vol. 30, part 1, 417.

4. Longstreet, *From Manassas to Appomattox*, 449.

5. McElroy, *Chickamauga*, 124.

6. Hill, "Chickamauga," 664.

7. Dana, *Recollections of the Civil War*, 115–16

8. O.R., vol. 30, part 2, 457.

North Dyer Field

1. O.R., vol. 30, part 1, 417, 441; O.R., vol. 30, part 2, 518; Longstreet, *From Manassas to Appomattox*, 448; McElroy, *Chickamauga*, 441. The 105th Ohio Regiment, credited by Reynolds for the bayonet charge when Union units collapsed at Poe farm, reported a bayonet charge on S. A. M. Wood's brigade of Cleburne's command.

2. O.R., vol. 30, part 1, 610, 623.

3. Ibid., 636–37; O.R., vol. 30, part 2, 511–12.

4. O.R., vol. 30, part 2, 503–4; O.R., vol. 30, part 1, 637.

5. O.R., vol. 30, part 1, 402.

Snodgrass Hill—Opening Moves

1. At the outset, Brannan's line consisted of the four brigades of Connell, Croxton, Harker, and Buell, some incomplete, with additional fragments of Van Cleve's and Negley's commands. Later arrivals included the brigades of Stanley, part of Sirwell's, Van Derveer's, and Hazen's, and the two brigades of Steedman's division.

2. Anderson, "The Campaign and Battle of Chickamauga," 414.

3. O.R., vol. 30, part 1, 253.

4. Ibid., 430.

5. Ibid., 252; O.R., vol. 30, part 2, 504.

6. O.R., vol. 30, part 2, 509.

7. Ibid., 504.

8. "Families of Chickamauga," historical files, CCNMP.

9. O.R., vol. 30, part 1, 637.

10. Robertson, *Staff Ride Handbook*, 136.

Tennessee Artillery Monument—
Forrest's Defense and Granger's Approach

1. O.R., vol. 30, part 1, 854–55, 862; O.R., vol. 30, part 2, 525.

2. Robertson, *Staff Ride Handbook*, 4, 18.

3. O.R., vol. 30, part 1, 860; O.R., vol. 30, part 2, 525.

Horseshoe Ridge—the Climactic Struggle

1. O.R., vol. 30, part 2, 504; McElroy, *Chickamauga*, 46; Belknap, *History*, 116–17.

2. *Battles and Leaders of the Civil War*, no. 23 of 32 parts (New York: Century Co., 1884), 667; O.R., vol. 30, part 2, 318, 460–62; O.R., vol. 30, part 1, 855, 860, 862–63.

3. O.R., vol. 30, part 1, 430, 763–64.

4. Longstreet, *From Manassas to Appomattox*, 450–54.

5. *Battles and Leaders*, 667; O.R., vol. 30, part 1, 253–54; O.R., vol. 30, part 2, 156, 364.

6. McElroy, *Chickamauga*, 56–57.

7. Paige and Greene, *Administrative History*.

8. McElroy, *Chickamauga*, 46–47; Belknap, *History*, 148–50.

9. O.R., vol. 30, part 2, 421.

10. Ibid., 461–62, 475.

11. Ibid.

12. Ibid., 459.

Kelly Farm to McFarland's Gap—Closing of the Battle

1. O.R., vol. 30, part 1, 79, 525.

2. *Battles and Leaders of the Civil War*, no. 23 of 32 parts (New York: Century Co., 1884), 661; O.R., vol. 30, part 2, 177–78, 184; O.R., vol. 30, part 1, 715.

3. O.R., vol. 30, part 1, 253–54.

Conclusion and Aftermath

1. Robertson, *Staff Ride Handbook*, 55.

2. Longstreet, *From Manassas to Appomattox*, 461–62; O.R., vol. 30, part 2, 34–35, 37.

3. *Battles and Leaders of the Civil War*, no. 23 of 32 parts (New York: Century Co., 1884), 662.

Abbazia, Patrick. *The Chickamauga Campaign*. Bryn Mawr: Combined Books, 1988.

Anderson, Archer. "The Campaign and Battle of Chickamauga." Vol. 9. Southern Historical Society Papers, 1881, 414.

Arnold, James R. *Chickamauga 1863: The River of Death*. London: Osprey/Reed International Books, 1997.

August Bratnober Account. Unit Files. Chickamauga and Chattanooga National Military Park, Fort Oglethorpe, Ga.

Battlefields in Dixie Land and Chickamauga National Military Park. Booklet produced for the Nashville, Chattanooga, and St. Louis Railroads and the Western and Atlantic Railroad. Chicago: Poole Brothers, 1928.

Baumgartner, Richard A. *Blue Lightning: Wilder's Mounted Infantry Brigade in the Battle of Chickamauga*. Huntington, W.Va.: Blue Acorn Press, 1997.

Baumgartner, Richard A., and Larry Strayer. *Echoes of Battle: The Struggle for Chattanooga*. Huntington, W.Va.: Blue Acorn Press, 1996.

Belknap, Charles E. *History of the Michigan Organizations at Chickamauga, Chattanooga, and Missionary Ridge—1863*. Lansing, Mich.: Robert Smith Printing Co., 1899.

Bennett, Lyman G. *History of the Thirty-sixth Regiment Illinois Volunteers during the War of the Great Rebellion*. Aurora, Ill.: Knickerbocker and Hodder, 1876.

Betts, Edward E., and Daniel S. Lamont. *Map of the Battlefield of Chickamauga*. N.p.: Chickamauga and Chattanooga National Park Commission, 1896.

Bowers, John. *Chickamauga and Chattanooga: The Battles That Doomed the Confederacy*. New York: Harper Collins Publishers, 1994.

Boynton, H. V. *The Chickamauga National Military Park: An Historical Guide, with Maps and Illustrations*. Cincinnati: Robert Clarke Co., 1895.

———. *Dedication of the Chickamauga and Chattanooga National Military Park, September 18–20, 1895*. Washington, D.C.: Government Printing Office, 1896.

Brown, Joseph M. *The Mountain Campaigns in Georgia*. Buffalo: Matthews, Northrup and Co., 1885.

Cist, Henry M. *The Army of the Cumberland*. New York: Charles Scribner's Sons, 1882.

Cleaves, Freeman. *Rock of Chickamauga: The Life of General George H. Thomas*. Norman: University of Oklahoma Press, 1948.

Connelly, Thomas Lawrence. *Autumn of Glory: The Army of Tennessee, 1862–1865*. Baton Rouge: Louisiana State University Press, 1971.

Cozzens, Peter. *This Terrible Sound: The Battle of Chickamauga*. Urbana: University of Illinois Press, 1992.

Dana, Charles A. *Recollections of the Civil War*. New York: Boughmans, 1898.

Daniel, Larry J. *Cannoneers in Gray: The Field Artillery of the Army of Tennessee, 1861–1865*. Tuscaloosa: University of Alabama Press, 1984.

Downey, Fairfax. *Storming of the Gateway: Chattanooga, 1863*. New York: David McKay Company, 1960.

Foote, Shelby. *The Civil War: A Narrative*. New York: Random House, 1963.

Gibson, J. T. *History of the Seventy-eighth Pennsylvania Volunteer Infantry*. Pittsburgh: Pittsburgh Printing, 1905.

Gracie, Archibald. *The Truth about Chickamauga*. Boston: Houghton, Mifflin, and Co., 1911.

Green, Francis Arthur. *The Witness of a House*. Chickamauga, Ga.: Gordon-Lee House, 1984.

Hallock, Judith L. *Braxton Bragg and Confederate Defeat*. Vol. 2. Tuscaloosa: University of Alabama Press, 1991.

Hill, D. H. "Chickamauga: The Great Battle of the West." *Battles and Leaders of the Civil War*. No. 23 of 32 parts. New York: Century Co., 1884.

Hollister, John J. *Chickamauga and Chattanooga on Your Own*. N.p.: Battlefield Guide Publishers, 1981.

Horn, Stanley F. *The Army of Tennessee*. Norman: University of Oklahoma Press, 1952.

Indiana at Chickamauga: 1863. Report of Indiana Commissioners (1900)—Chickamauga National Military Park. Indianapolis: Wm. B. Burford, 1901.

Indianapolis Daily Journal, Sept. 28, 1863.

Johnson, Curt, and Mark McLaughlin. *Civil War Battles*. New York: Fairfax Press, 1977.

Korn, Jerry. *The Fight for Chattanooga: Chickamauga to Missionary Ridge*. Alexandria, Va.: Time-Life Books, Inc., 1985.

Longstreet, James. *From Manassas to Appomattox*. Philadelphia: J. B. Lippincott Company, 1895.

Lynde, Francis. *Battles of Chattanooga and Vicinity: A Monograph*. Chattanooga: Chattanooga Community Association, ca. 1930.

McDonough, James Lee. *Chattanooga: A Death Grip on the Confederacy*. Knoxville: University of Tennessee Press, 1984.

McElfresh, Earl B. *Maps and Mapmakers of the Civil War*. New York: Harry N. Abrams, in association with History Book Club, 1999.

McElroy, Joseph C. *Chickamauga: Record of the Ohio Chickamauga and Chattanooga National Park Commission*. Cincinnati: Earhart and Richardson, 1896.

McKinney, Francis F. *Education in Violence: The Life of George H. Thomas and the History of the Army of the Cumberland*. Detroit: Wayne State University Press, 1961.

Minnich, J. W. *Unique Experiences in the Chickamauga Campaign*. Confederate Veteran, vol. 35. Nashville: Trustees of the Confederate Veteran, 1927.

Morrison, Larry A., and Bruce W. Eppinette. *Historical Ouachita County: A Photographic Collection*. Camden, Ark.: Southern Arkansas University Tech, 1986.

Moulton, Gary E. *John Ross: Cherokee Chief*. Athens: University of Georgia Press, 1986.

Norwood, C. W., comp. *Book of Battles: Chickamauga and Chattanooga Campaigns and Battle-Fields*. Chattanooga: Gervis M. Connelly Co., 1898.

Paige, John C., and Jerome A. Greene, *Administrative History of Chickamauga and Chattanooga National Military Park*. Denver: National Park Service, 1983.

Piston, William G. *Lee's Tarnished Lieutenant: James Longstreet and His Place in Southern History*. Athens: University of Georgia Press, 1987.

Polley, Joseph B. *Hood's Texas Brigade: Its Marches, Its Battles, Its Achievements*. New York: Neale, 1910.

Ray, Frederick E. *"Our Special Artist": Alfred R. Waud's Civil War*. Mechanicsburg, Pa.: Stackpole Books, 1994.

Robertson, William G. *The Battle of Chickamauga: Eastern National Civil War Series*. Conshohocken, Pa.: Eastern National, 1995.

Robertson, William Glenn, et al. *Staff Ride Handbook for the Battle of Chickamauga*. Fort Leavenworth: Combat Studies Institute/U.S. Army Command and General Staff College, 1992.

Sidebottom, A. W. *The "Boys" in Camp Thomas/Chickamauga and Chattanooga National Military Park, Georgia*. Chattanooga: Sidebottom and Kerr, 1898.

Skinner, George W., ed. *Pennsylvania at Chickamauga and Chattanooga: Ceremonies at the Dedication of the Monuments Erected by the Commonwealth of Pennsylvania*. N.p.: William Stanley Ray, State Printer of Pennsylvania, 1901.

Society of the Army of the Cumberland, Twenty-third Reunion—Chickamauga, Ga. Cincinnati: Robert Clarke Co., 1892.

Sorrell, Moxley. *Recollections of a Confederate Staff Officer*. New York: Neale, 1905.

Souvenir Album of Lookout Mountain, Chickamauga and Chattanooga National Military Park. Chattanooga: T. H. Payne and Co., ca. 1902.

Spruill, Matt, ed. *Guide to the Battle of Chickamauga*. Lawrence: University Press of Kansas, 1993.

Sullivan, James R. *Chickamauga and Chattanooga Battlefields*. No. 25. Washington, D.C.: National Park Service Historical Handbook, 1956.

Sword, Wiley. *Mountains Touched with Fire*. New York: St. Martin's Press, 1995.

Trowbridge, J. T. *A Picture of the Desolated States; and the Work of Restoration: 1865–1868*. Hartford: L. Stebbins, 1868.

Tucker, Glenn. *The Battle of Chickamauga*. Harrisburg, Pa.: Historical Times Inc., 1969. Reprint, [Conshohocken, Pa.?]: Eastern Acorn Press, 1981.

———. *Chickamauga: Bloody Battle in the West*. Indianapolis: Bobbs-Merrill Co., 1961.

The War of the Rebellion: A Compilation of the Official Records of the Union and Confederate Armies. Washington, D.C.: U.S. Government Printing Office, 1880–1901.

Watkins, Sam R. *"Co. Aytch": A Side Show of the Big Show*. New York: Collier Books, 1974.

Wilson, James H. *Under the Old Flag*. New York: D. Appleton and Co., 1912.

Woodhead, Henry, ed. *Voices of the Civil War: Chickamauga*. Alexandria: Time-Life Books, 1997.

Woodworth, Steven E. *Chickamauga: A Battlefield Guide*. New York: University of Nebraska Press, 1999.

———. *Six Armies in Tennessee: The Chickamauga and Chattanooga Campaigns*. New York: University of Nebraska Press, 1998.

PHOTOGRAPH AND ILLUSTRATION CREDITS

Photographs with no listed credit are by the author.

iii: From *Battles and Leaders of the Civil War*, no. 23 of 32 parts (New York: Century Co., 1884).

v: CCNMP.

xii: USGS, LandNet Corporation, www.landnetusa.com

6: From *Battles and Leaders of the Civil War*, no. 23 of 32 parts (New York: Century Co., 1884).

8: From *Society of the Army of the Cumberland*.

9: NA, 111-B-7026.

11, top: NA, 111-B-4791.

11, bottom: NA, 111-B-4811.

14, left: NA, 111-B-547.

14, right: NA, 111-B-7039.

17, left: From Boynton, *Dedication*.

17, right: LC.

18, bottom: From Belknap, *History*.

20: From Boynton, *Dedication*.

25, left: CCNMP.

25, right: Photograph by Emmett L. Given, Huntsville, Alabama.

28: From McElroy, *Chickamauga*.

30: From Boynton, *Chickamauga Guide*.

31: From Boynton, *Chickamauga Guide*.

32, top: Emmett L. Given.

32, bottom: Chickamauga and Chattanooga National Park Commission, "Map of the Battlefield of Chickamauga," no. 1, Edward E. Betts, C.E., Park Engineer, 1896. Courtesy of the National Park Service.

33: NA, 111-B-4857.

34: Ouachita County (AR) Historic Photograph Collection, Southern Arkansas University Tech, Camden, Arkansas.

36, left: Emmett L. Given.

36, right: A. R. Waud, Hulton Archive/ Getty Images.

38, bottom: Emmett L. Given.

39: Mass. Commander/Military Order of the Loyal Legion—Carlisle Barracks/ USAMHI.

42, left: Emmett L. Given.

42, right: LC, LC-D4-39511.

44, right: From Skinner, ed., *Pennsylvania at Chickamauga*.

46, left: Emmett L. Given.

46, right: Edward E. Betts, "Map of the Battlefield of Chickamauga," no. 1, Brock field area. Courtesy of the National Park Service.

47, left: From McElroy, *Chickamauga*.

48, left: From the author's collection.

50: Emmett L. Given.

52: From Boynton, *Dedication*.

58, top: From *Indiana at Chickamauga*.

58, bottom: From an original 1900 class photograph, W. F. Dailey, teacher. Courtesy of Gladys Dailey Nevels, Sale City, Georgia.

59: From Baumgartner, *Blue Lightning*. Courtesy of Eli Lilly and Company Archives, Indianapolis.

60: Emmett L. Given.

62, right: LC, LC-DRWG/US-Waud (W), no. 34.

64: From Boynton, *Chickamauga Guide*.

65: From Boynton, *Chickamauga Guide*.

66, left: Emmett L. Given.

67: From Boynton, *Chickamauga Guide*.

69, right: CCNMP.

71: Emmett L. Given.

72, left: CCNMP.

73, right: Rotograph Co., New York, 1907.

75, right: Photo by Emmett L. Given.

76, right: From Boynton, *Dedication*.

79: CCNMP.

80, left: Alfred Waud print, from *Battlefields in Dixie Land*.

82: CCNMP.

84, right: From Boynton, *Dedication*.

85: Postcard, W. M. Cline Company, Chattanooga, Tennessee, n.d.

86: From *Souvenir Album*.

89: From Skinner, ed., *Pennsylvania at Chickamauga*.

93: NA, 111-B-4811.

95: From Boynton, *Chickamauga Guide*.

97: From *Society of the Army of the Cumberland*.

101: Emmett L. Given.

102: Frank Vitzetelly print, by permission of the Houghton Library, Harvard University, pfMS Am 1585 (25).

105: Courtesy of USAMHI.

106: From Boynton, *Dedication*.

108, right: Courtesy of Dan Hatzenbuehler, Hatzenbuehler Photography, Dallas, Texas. Copyright 1998 Dan Hatzenbuehler.

112: From *Souvenir Album*.

113: *Battlefields in Dixie Land*.

114, left: CCNMP.

114, right: From Skinner, ed., *Pennsylvania at Chickamauga*.

115, left: From Boynton, *Chickamauga Guide*.

115, right: CCNMP.

116–17: Panoramic postcard, n.d., n.p.

119: CCNMP.

120: Emmett L. Given.